D0073473

A PHILOSOPHY
OF INDIVIDUAL
FREEDOM

Recent Titles in
Contributions in Political Science
Series Editor: Bernard K. Johnpoll

A PHILOSOPHY OF INDIVIDUAL FREEDOM

The Political Thought of F. A. Hayek

CALVIN M. HOY

Contributions in Political Science, Number 119

GREENWOOD PRESS
Westport, Connecticut · London, England

Library of Congress Cataloging in Publication Data

Hoy, Calvin M.
  A philosophy of individual freedom.

  (Contributions in political science, ISSN 0147-1066 ;
no. 119)
  Bibliography: p.
  Includes index.
  1. Hayek, Friedrich A. von (Friedrich August von),
1899–   —Political science. 2. Liberty. I. Title.
II. Series.
JC273.H382H69   1985   320'.01   84-8973
ISBN 0-313-24361-1 (lib. bdg.)

Copyright © 1984 by Calvin M. Hoy

All rights reserved. No portion of this book may be
reproduced, by any process or technique, without the
express written consent of the publisher.

Library of Congress Catalog Card Number: 84-8973
ISBN: 0-313-24361-1
ISSN: 0147-1066

First published in 1984

Greenwood Press
A division of Congressional Information Service, Inc.
88 Post Road West
Westport, Connecticut 06881

Printed in the United States of America

10 9 8 7 6 5 4 3 2 1

Copyright Acknowledgments

The author wishes to thank the University of Chicago Press, and Routledge & Kegan Paul, London, for the use of excerpts from the following works:

Friedrich A. Hayek, *The Road to Serfdom,* © 1944 by The University of Chicago. By permission of the University of Chicago Press for rights in the United States and Canada, and Routledge & Kegan Paul for world rights outside the United States and Canada.

Friedrich A. Hayek, *Individualism and Economic Order,* Copyright © 1948 by The University of Chicago. By permission of the University of Chicago Press for rights in the United States and Canada, and Routledge & Kegan Paul for world rights outside the United States and Canada.

Friedrich A. Hayek, *The Constitution of Liberty,* Copyright © 1960 by The University of Chicago. By permission of the University of Chicago Press for rights in the United States and Canada, and Routledge & Kegan Paul for world rights outside the United States and Canada.

F. A. Hayek, *Studies in Philosophy, Politics and Economics,* Copyright © 1967 by F. A. Hayek. By permission of the University of Chicago Press for rights in the United States, and Routledge & Kegan Paul for world rights outside the United States.

F. A. Hayek, *New Studies in Philosophy, Politics, and Economics and the History of Ideas,* © 1978 by F. A. Hayek. By permission of the University of Chicago Press for rights in the United States and Canada, and Routledge & Kegan Paul for world rights outside the United States and Canada.

F. A. Hayek, *Rules and Order,* Vol. 1 of *Law, Legislation and Liberty,* © 1973 by F. A. Hayek. By permission of the University of Chicago Press for rights in the United States and Canada, and Routledge & Kegan Paul for world rights outside the United States and Canada.

F. A. Hayek, *The Mirage of Social Justice,* Vol. 2 of *Law, Legislation and Liberty,* © 1976 by F. A. Hayek. By permission of the University of Chicago Press for rights in the United States and Canada, and Routledge & Kegan Paul for world rights outside the United States and Canada.

F. A. Hayek, *The Political Order of a Free People,* Vol. 3 of *Law, Legislation and Liberty,* © 1979 by F. A. Hayek. By permission of the University of Chicago Press for rights in the United States and Canada, and Routledge & Kegan Paul for world rights outside the United States and Canada.

Milton Friedman, *Capitalism and Freedom,* © 1962 by The University of Chicago. By permission of the University of Chicago Press for world rights.

In honor of my mother,
Lucille Hoy,
and
in memory of my father,
Meirl C. Hoy

Contents

Acknowledgments

In the preparation of this volume I have benefited from the assistance of a number of individuals. William Nattrass and David Gillespie were each kind enough to procure a source for me. Several chapters from an early version of the work were read and reviewed by James F. Gill. Professor Julian H. Franklin and Professor Herbert A. Deane each read several early drafts in entirety and contributed many useful suggestions. Arthur J. Brahm reviewed an early draft of the work as well as the penultimate copy. My greatest debts are due to Lucille Hoy, who patiently typed and retyped successive early versions, and also assisted in the proofreading, and to Kathy Zirkel, who painstakingly typed the final copy. Each of these individuals has helped to make this volume more intelligible than would otherwise be the case, and I thank them for their efforts.

A PHILOSOPHY
OF INDIVIDUAL
FREEDOM

I.

An Introduction

Born on May 8, 1899, in Vienna, Friedrich August von Hayek earned a Doctor of Law degree in 1921, and a Doctor of Political Science degree in 1923, both at the University of Vienna. Hayek's family contains a rather large number of academicians: his father, two grandfathers, two brothers, daughter, and son have been scientists and teachers, though, unlike Friedrich Hayek, most of them have been physical scientists.

From 1927 to 1931, Hayek was Director of the Austrian Institute for Economic Research, and from 1929 to 1931 a Lecturer in Economics at the University of Vienna. He served as Tooke Professor of Economic Science and Statistics, from 1931 to 1950, at the University of London. In 1950, he became Professor of Social and Moral Science at the University of Chicago. He left the University of Chicago in 1962 to take the position of Professor of Economics at the University of Freiburg, from which he retired in 1967. Until 1974, Hayek served as a Visiting Professor at the University of Salzburg.[1] Since 1974, Hayek has been active in academic circles, as his publications indicate.

Hayek's publications indicate a variety of interests in the social sciences: psychology,[2] the philosophy of the social sciences,[3] and history (especially intellectual history).[4] However, he began his career as an economist, and his early works in economics earned him the Alfred Nobel Memorial Prize in Economic Sciences in 1974.[5]

Besides his interest in the subjects mentioned, Hayek has, at least since the late 1930s, written extensively in the field of political philosophy,[6] and it is this aspect of his work that we shall be concerned with here. The theme of Hayek's political philosophy is that individual liberty is being destroyed, unintentionally, and that it is only our adherence to certain principles that will prevent the destruction of liberty.

Due to his concern for the survival of individual freedom, in April 1947 Hayek founded the Mont Pelerin Society. This association's basic purpose is to provide a sympathetic forum for the discussion and elaboration of the principles of classical liberalism.[7]

Moreover, Hayek's concern for the preservation of individual liberty has led him to attempt a "comprehensive restatement of the basic principles of a philosophy of freedom."[8] In this work, we shall attempt to explicate Hayek's philosophy of freedom, and we shall examine his claim to have stated a comprehensive philosophy of liberty.

An examination of Hayek's political philosophy is pertinent for several reasons. First, the pursuit of individual liberty is a noble pursuit, and the preservation of liberty is of interest to more than a narrow circle of people. Second, Hayek is an important social theorist who expounds a rather consistent philosophy of freedom that is based on market economics, and in particular on the function of prices. Third, some of the tracts that have been written on Hayek's political thought seem to be over-critical of Hayek. Note Herman Finer's *The Road to Reaction,* where the mere title suggests an unsympathetic examination of Hayek's philosophy. In his preface, Finer says that he will prove

that Hayek's apparatus of learning is deficient, his reading incomplete; that his understanding of the economic process is bigoted, his account of history false; that his political science is almost non-existent, his terminology misleading, his comprehension of British and American political procedure and mentality gravely defective; and that his attitude to average men and women is truculently authoritarian.[9]

Christian Bay entitled his article "Hayek's Liberalism: The Constitution of Perpetual Privilege." He was going to call it "Social Darwinism with a Human Face," but he found that title to be too generous because "there is not very much concern for human beings in Hayek's philosophy of liberty."[10]

In chapter two of this book, we shall analyze Hayek's definition of freedom and state the reasons why he believes individual liberty is valuable. In chapters three, four, and five, we shall discover his methods for preserving liberty. In particular, the third chapter will examine the type of economic system he believes is essential to freedom. The fourth chapter will explain the relationship that Hayek perceives between law and liberty. In the fifth chapter, we shall ascertain and examine his views on how government should be structured in order to preserve liberty. The sixth and final chapter will attempt to determine whether or not Hayek has articulated a comprehensive statement on individual liberty.

TWO TRADITIONS OF POLITICAL DISCOURSE

Before beginning our inquiry into Hayek's philosophy of freedom, a discussion of two topics will help us put Hayek's political thought into perspective. Hayek divides philosophy (or at least modern philosophy) into two types, constructivist rationalism and evolutionary rationalism.[11] René Descartes, Thomas Hobbes, Jean-Jacques Rousseau, and Jeremy Bentham are described by Hayek as constructivist rationalists. Among philosophers that Hayek classifies as evolutionary rationalists are Adam Smith, Edmund Burke, Bernard Mandeville, and Alexis de Tocqueville. Apparently David Hume is the philosopher par excellence of this tradition.[12] Some philosophers, says Hayek, overlap both traditions, for instance, John Stuart Mill and Herbert Spencer.[13] This twofold division of philosophy seems to apply to mainly modern thought. Though Hayek does not appear to be entirely clear on this point, it seems that ancient and medieval theorists are merely precursors of one tradition or the other. For instance, Aristotle, Cicero, and Aquinas are forerunners of evolutionary rational-ism,[14] while Plato and (apparently) Augustine are, at least, forerunners of constructivist rationalism.[15]

According to Hayek, constructivist rationalism is a philo-sophical school that believes in applying deductive reasoning to human affairs. It believes in a human creator for society, language, and law. It also believes that as these institutions have been humanly created they can be refashioned or com-pletely changed by human beings following a rational design for human life. Socialist thought is a logical outgrowth of this tradition, and this tradition is highly criticized by Hayek.

Evolutionary rationalism, the tradition of discourse to which Hayek belongs, believes that society, language, and law de-velop in an evolutionary manner and are not designed by any-one and cannot be refashioned in any mode that deductive reasoning may suggest.

Hayek says that both of the traditions are utilitarian. They are different in this respect: the utilitarianism of the evolu-tionary rationalist is one of rules or principles. A particular rule is justified by its usefulness, but its usefulness is judged in regard to a series of cases. The utilitarianism of the con-structivist rationalist is a case by case method that dispenses with rules.[16] And, as we shall see, especially in chapter three, Hayek believes that the implications of evolutionary rational-ism are liberal and that the implications of constructivist ra-tionalism are totalitarian.

As one might almost expect, Hayek's scheme of classifica-tion has been accepted by some scholars and rejected by oth-ers. Ralf Dahrendorf says that he accepts Hayek's "analysis without reservation."[17] On the other hand, Eugene F. Miller does not totally accept Hayek's classification. Miller, however, does not completely dismiss Hayek's division of modern phi-losophy; he seems to restrict his objections to associating an-cient and medieval theorists with modern theorists. For ex-ample, Miller believes that, philosophically, Plato and Aristotle are more closely related to each other than either one is to Descartes or Hume.[18]

However, my purpose in presenting Hayek's system of clas-sification is not to accept or reject it as a useful or useless device in studying the history of philosophy. Rather, my intention is to put Hayek's political thought in perspective, that is, to show that Hayek believes his philosophy is closer to that of Hume, for example, than to Hobbes, that his philosophy is based on cultural evolution (though not biological evolution),[19] and that he believes that the implications of only one of these two modes of thought are liberal.

AN OLD WHIG

Though we have described Hayek as a member of a tradition of philosophical discourse that he chooses to call evolutionary rationalism, in regard to contemporary political doctrines Hayek labels himself an "Old Whig." Though modern political thought is often referred to as either conservative or liberal, Hayek is reluctant to use either term to describe his position. He would prefer to call himself a liberal (in the classical sense), but he feels that he cannot do this because the term has been preempted by radicals and socialists. Some classical liberals refer to themselves as libertarians; however, Hayek finds this term unattractive. Though in the United States some classical liberals refer to themselves as conservatives, Hayek does not want to use this term to describe his political philosophy because it has a very different connotation in Europe. Many Continental conservatives, says Hayek, are fearful of change, too distrustful of democracy, and too nationalistic. Historically, says Hayek, it was the Whig party that represented the ideals of individual liberty, and it is these ideals that he is most interested in preserving. Thus, Hayek concludes that he is "simply an unrepentant Old Whig—with the stress on the 'old.'"[20]

NOTES

1. The information on Hayek's life can be found in Machlup, 1976b, pp. 13–15, as well as in almost any publication of Hayek's by the Institute of Economic Affairs, e.g., Hayek, 1980, p. 10.
2. See Hayek, 1952b.
3. See Hayek, 1952a.

4. See Hayek, 1954b, and Hayek, 1951b.

5. His early economic treatises include Hayek, 1933a; Hayek, 1935e; Hayek, 1937b; Hayek, 1939e; Hayek, 1941b. On Hayek's technical economics see O'Driscoll, 1977, and Machlup, 1976b.

6. See Hayek, 1939c.

7. See Machlup, 1976a, pp. xi-xiv, and Hayek, 1967b, pp. 148–159.

8. Hayek, 1960a, p. 3.

9. Finer, 1963, p. vii. Also see Seligman, 1962, p. 827 n. 445.

10. Bay, 1971, pp. 93–94.

11. For Hayek's discussion of these different philosophical traditions, see Hayek, 1946; Hayek, 1958b; Hayek, 1960a, pp. 54–71; Hayek, 1965; Hayek, 1966d; Hayek, 1967b, pp. 96–105; Hayek, 1973c, pp. 1–54; Hayek, 1976e, pp. 17–24; Hayek, 1978c, pp. 119–151.

12. Hayek has a very high regard for Hume. See Hayek, 1960a, p. 420 n. 9.

13. Hayek, 1948, p. 11.

14. Hayek, 1967b, p. 94.

15. On Plato see Hayek, 1976e, p. 105. On Augustine see Hayek, 1979, p. 166.

16. See Hayek, 1960a, p. 159; Hayek, 1967b, p. 88; Hayek, 1976e, p. 19. Though it may appear odd for Hayek to include, e.g., Plato in a utilitarian tradition, he appears to do this because Plato would judge cases on their individual merits.

17. Dahrendorf, 1968, p. 220.

18. Miller, 1979, pp. 251, 266–267.

19. See Hayek, 1979, pp. 153–176.

20. Hayek, 1960a, p. 409.

II.

The Meaning and Value of Freedom

In this chapter, we shall primarily be interested in determining what Hayek means by freedom and why he regards individual liberty as a desirable condition for rational and responsible human beings.[1]

FREEDOM: A PRELIMINARY DEFINITION

Though Hayek is an intense advocate of individual liberty, he does not believe that there ever was or will be a state of perfect freedom. For Hayek, freedom is negative; it is merely the absence of coercion. Freedom, or liberty (he uses the terms synonymously), refers to relations among men.[2]

Freedom can be achieved only relatively because the state must possess coercive powers to prevent individuals from exercising coercion. A coercive apparatus must always exist if only to prevent more severe coercion.[3] Thus, Hayek's definition of a state of freedom is "that condition of men in which coercion of some by others is reduced as much as is possible in society."[4]

In describing liberty, he might have used, he tells us, the words restraint or constraint rather than coercion. He did not do so because neither of these terms so nearly implies a human cause as does coercion.[5] As an example, Hayek says that if a mountain climber falls into a crevasse and cannot extricate himself, he cannot be said to be unfree, or to have lost his liberty. His physical condition may prevent him from doing as he likes, but no one is forcing him to do anything or preventing him from doing anything.[6]

Though the term coercion is preferable to the words restraint or constraint for expressing what he means by an unfree condition, it does not fully express what he means. Normally, coercion only implies compulsion. Hayek means to say that an unfree state is one in which an individual is not only forced into a particular act but prevented from performing a particular act. Thus, in a sense, freedom is the absence of both coercion and restraint. Hayek, though, settles on using the word coercion to contrast with liberty, with the proviso that coercion means prevention as well as compulsion. However, whatever term is chosen to contrast with liberty it must not only convey the ideas of prevention and compulsion but it must also imply a human cause.[7]

There is some ambiguity in Hayek's presentation of his definition, that is, it is not exactly clear whether he intends to present his definition as the true meaning of the word or merely as the definition he intends to use. In *Freedom,* Maurice Cranston explains that there are two ways of defining terms, *stipulative* and *lexicographical.* Stipulative definitions are arbitrary: terms are defined merely by stipulating, or asserting, that they will be used in a particular sense. Lexicographical definitions are either true or false: they do not merely stipulate that a word will be used in a particular sense but they "report the way words are conventionally used."[8] Hayek starts out with a stipulative definition and even criticizes attempts at a lexicographical definition.[9] Yet he seems to slip into using a type of definition that is not altogether different from what Cranston refers to as lexicographical. Almost immediately after criticizing attempts to discover the literal meaning of freedom, Hayek says that his definition "seems to be the original meaning of the word" and that throughout history the distinction between a free man and an unfree man "had a very definite meaning."[10] Despite Hayek's initial avowal to avoid a discussion of what freedom really means, he claims far more for his definition than that it is a stipulative one.

THREE ALTERNATIVE DEFINITIONS

Though Hayek defines freedom as the absence of coercion, he observes that freedom is not always defined in contrast to coercion. He examines three other common definitions of freedom to show that they are distinct from his own definition (which, for clarity, I will occasionally refer to as individual or negative liberty).

The first definition Hayek calls inner freedom. This means that one is free only if one does what one ought to do. According to this definition of freedom, one is not free if he follows his impulses rather than his considered reason. One is not a free man simply by virtue of being left to his own judgments. The absence of coercion, in this view, may, though it need not, be a condition of freedom but it is not a complete condition. Besides being free from others, one must be free from his passions as well. Slavery resides just as much in domination by one's passions as in coercion.

Though Plato did not exactly phrase his arguments in the following manner, for the purpose of illustration his position will be regarded as if he did.[11] Man's psyche, for Plato, is divided into three parts: reason, spirit, and appetite. The appetites, or passions, are desires that seek satisfaction. The role of wisdom, or reason, is to control the passions and spirit. The passions may prod one to commit an evil act that is immediately perceived as good. Reason does not aid the passions in satisfying this desire but attempts to squelch it. If passion rules, one is continually doing something that may not only be evil, but something that one really does not wish to do at all. If one does what one does not want to do, in what sense is one free?

This definition of freedom can apply to a solitary individual. One could have a passion for food to the degree that he eats until he becomes sick. It cannot be held that under normal circumstances one should or would want to make oneself ill. If one acts so as to do this, it must be concluded that he is working toward an end that he does not want to achieve. If one does what one does not want to do, one is not free. Hayek does not regard this dilemma between passion and reason in terms of freedom or a lack of freedom.

Hayek believes inner freedom is related to individual freedom, though they are not identical. According to Hayek, if individual freedom is the absence of coercion, freedom and coercion are opposites. Moral weakness, not coercion, is the opposite of inner freedom. Since moral weakness and coercion are not the same, it follows that inner freedom and individual freedom are not the same.[12] Inner freedom is related to freedom insofar as the severity of coercion is a relative phenomenon. Perhaps an example is the best explanation.

X asks Y to rob a bank with him. Y refuses, saying that in his considered judgment such an act is evil. X threatens Y with the loss of his friendship unless Y joins him. Overcome by the passion for X's friendship, Y assents to the act. According to the definition of inner freedom, Y is not a free agent. His reason has been overcome by his passion. He has decided to act against his true will, or against what he ought to do.

Has Y been coerced? I am confident that Hayek would answer that he has not. He would doubtlessly fault him for being morally weak, but he would argue that courage and freedom are merely related and not synonymous.[13] The important point here is that what one person may perceive as coercion may not be considered coercion by another. It is possible that Y, in the example above, may feel more pressure, or coercion, than would another individual even if in a similar situation he was threatened with the loss of life. Inner freedom, according to Hayek, is related to freedom insofar as an individual has the determination and will to pursue his own course of action. Strength of will may determine to what degree one uses his freedom, but individual freedom exists independently of will.[14]

The second definition of freedom that Hayek contrasts to his own is political freedom. According to this definition, one is free insofar as one participates in making collective, or governmental, decisions. The ability to vote for government policies is often the criterion by which one is judged to be free. Among political philosophers, Rousseau seems to adopt a definition of liberty that closely resembles the one we have just described. In a country that is commonly thought to be free, Rousseau says that the citizens of England are free only at the time of elections. He argues that freedom means obeying a law that one himself has made.[15]

Though freedom is sometimes defined as political participation, or, what is essentially the same thing, democracy, Hayek does not identify individual liberty with political freedom because there are people that cannot vote and yet are free, for example, residents of the District of Columbia. Not only does Hayek refuse to identify political liberty with individual liberty, he also argues that political liberty can completely abridge individual liberty. An individual, says Hayek, may vote himself into slavery and thus give up his freedom.[16]

Isaiah Berlin has, within the last several decades, taken up the problem of the relationship between voting and freedom. He also argues that the two are not synonymous and that political liberty can negate freedom. He says, and with a great deal of merit, that anything one finds desirable one seems to label freedom. Political participation may be good, and the lack of it bad, but that does not mean it is freedom. The difference between the two is that political liberty answers the question, "By whom am I governed?" while the other answers the question, "How much am I governed?"[17]

Positive freedom is the third definition of freedom that Hayek contrasts to his own. Unlike the other definitions of freedom, positive freedom, according to Hayek, is rather modern.[18]

This definition of freedom particularly attracts the ire of Hayek. He believes that it can be used to demand a redistribution of wealth and he closely associates it with socialism.[19] According to this definition, freedom is something that is at least akin to power, wealth, or ability. It is not enough to say that someone is free to purchase a yacht simply because no one restrains another from such a purchase. If one does not have, say, the wealth to make such a purchase, one is not free to make such a purchase. Hayek refers to this definition of freedom as the most dangerous one. And whereas he at least tolerates the other two definitions that he distinguishes from his own, he does not do so in regard to positive liberty.[20]

In a sense, both positive liberty and negative liberty are defined as the absence of restraint. Hayek distinguishes his own definition of liberty from positive liberty by pointing out that according to the latter a deprivation of freedom would not be limited to force or prevention due to human beings but would refer to any external impediment, human or not. Thus, freedom is interpreted "as effective power to do whatever we want." And this, in turn, "inevitably leads to the identification of liberty with wealth."[21] Hayek argues that wealth and power are not identical to liberty and that it is possible for "the penniless vagabond" to be "freer than the conscripted soldier with all his security and relative comfort."[22]

Before we leave Hayek's discussion of positive freedom, a brief explanation of his thoughts on power and wealth, and especially the former, is necessary. Though Hayek frowns on the identification of either wealth or power with freedom, he does not think that either wealth or power is inherently evil. He refers to liberty and wealth as both being "good things."[23] But a slight problem arises with his use of the word power. He argues that power is not necessarily an evil because there are two types of power: power over things and power over people. Political theorists like Edmund Burke and Lord Acton were mistaken to regard power as the supreme evil. He says "it is not power as such-the capacity to achieve what one wants-that is bad, but only the power to coerce, to force other men to serve one's will by the threat of inflicting harm."[24] Thus, for Hayek, power is "the capacity to achieve what one wants" and as such is good. What Hayek regards as evil is power over people. His use of the word power creates a slight difficulty on which I can comment only briefly. Power has not only been regarded as an evil by a number of political philosophers, as Hayek notes, but it is used by some contemporary political observers in merely a relational manner. Some political analysts use power solely as a relation between individuals and thus might possibly accuse Hayek of misusing the word. Harold Lasswell and Abraham Kaplan, in *Power and Society,* seem to make a distinction similar to Hayek's if only by stipulating that "political power is distinguished from power over nature as power over other men."[25] But Lasswell and Kaplan cite other authors that use the term purely in a relational sense.

Friedrich emphasizes this point by formulating as an "axiom" concerning power that "it is a certain kind of human relationship." Tawney's definition similarly restricts intended effects to those on the conduct of other persons: "Power may be defined as the capacity of an individual, or a group of individuals, to modify the conduct of other individuals or groups in the manner which he desires. . . ."[26]

Bertrand Russell, however, defines power much as Hayek does. He says, "power may be defined as the production of intended effects." And he also says that there are two types of power: "there is power over human beings and power over dead matter or non-human forms of life."[27] I do not mean to imply that Hayek misuses the word, but he could and should have made it clearer that his use of the word does not correspond to the way in which some political scientists use it.

THE MEANING OF FREEDOM ELABORATED

Hayek attempts to elaborate his definition of freedom by defining coercion more precisely. It seems that he has two reasons for expanding on his definition of coercion. First, he wants to broaden the meaning of coercion, and, second, he wants to limit the number of cases of coercion that the state must prevent.

As we have said, Hayek defines coercion as prevention and/or compulsion humanly caused. In another statement, he says "coercion implies both the threat of inflicting harm and the intention thereby to bring about certain conduct."[28] Thus, we can, I believe, say that according to Hayek a coercive act has two parts: a threat of harm, and, by this threat, the attempt to change an individual's behavior.

By thus defining coercion, we can separate it from violence and also broaden its meaning. According to this definition, we can conclude that not every act of violence is coercive. A mugging would certainly be an act of violence but it would not be a coercive act unless it is intended to impose a certain pattern of behavior on the victim, for example, compelling the victim to surrender his money.

But of far greater importance, for Hayek, than the separation of violence from coercion is its opposite, that is, just as every violent act is not necessarily coercive, so every coercive act is not necessarily violent. Hayek writes of one's mind being "made someone else's tool," and he appears to mean by this that under certain conditions someone can manipulate another's environment so drastically that without the threat of physical force the manipulator can cause the person being manipulated to carry out actions that are approved of by the former but not the latter.[29] Fraud, says Hayek, is somewhat analogous to this type of coercion.[30] If the necessary means for our actions are all controlled by another, this other person will be able to frustrate our ambitions.[31] To prevent this type of coercion, a private sphere is necessary. In essence, a private sphere means a demarcated area which the individual controls. It includes private property. Though it does not require that any particular individual necessarily possess property, it prevents coercion by preventing one other agent from possessing the sole control of material goods which are the means for our actions.[32]

Besides broadening the concept of coercion, Hayek attempts to restrict the number of cases of coercion which should be prevented by government. According to Hayek, coercion can be so broadly defined "as to make it an all-pervasive and unavoidable phenomenon." However, "there are many degrees of coercion" and we cannot prevent "all the milder forms of coercion," though we should "try to prevent all the more severe forms of coercion."[33] And even some of the severe forms of coercion, such as some arising from family relationships, cannot be prevented by the state, at least not without producing even more coercion. To illustrate cases of true coercion, Hayek says that true coercion consists of armed conquerors subjecting individuals to forced labor, or gangsters extorting a fee for protection.[34] The type of coercion that the state must prevent is that which "is likely to affect the normal, average person."[35]

A possible motive for Hayek's expatiations on his original definition of freedom is to allow him to show that freedom is inherent in a market economy and inherently absent in a non-market economy. Many of his examples, some of which we shall now examine, are based on economic considerations. Hayek goes to some trouble to demonstrate that the conditions under which individuals render services or benefits to others do not normally entail coercion. At least in a competitive market, a producer or dealer cannot coerce me if he refuses to sell me his goods or services except at a high price because I can always turn to someone else to supply these goods or services. Even under conditions of monopoly, the provider of a commodity or service cannot normally coerce me providing that these services "are not crucial to my existence or the preservation of what I most value."[36] For example, says Hayek, if a well-known artist refuses to paint someone's portrait unless he receives a high price, this would not be coercion.

On the employment side of the market, Hayek argues that an employer cannot coerce an employee as long as other employment opportunities exist. If, however, dismissal results in a diminution of income, the employer will have caused pain.[37] However, if we recall that Hayek divides a coercive act into two parts, a threat of harm and the intention to change conduct, it is not clear why he should not regard conditions of employment as at least potentially coercive. If an employer threatens harm (or pain), and intends thereby to change someone's conduct, this would, according to Hayek's description, be coercive. Since he assumes a market, that is, many employers, and since he attempts to distinguish between degrees of coercion, it would be more apt for him to describe such a condition as one of mild coercion, that is, one which will not affect the average individual, providing of course that the threat of a diminution of income will not affect such an individual.

Though the conditions of production and employment in a market are non-coercive, there are rare instances where the terms of exchange can be coercive. In an example that we shall refer to several times in this chapter, Hayek says,

a monopolist could exercise true coercion, however, if he were, say, the owner of a spring in an oasis. Let us say that other persons settled there on the assumption that water would always be available at a reasonable price and then found, perhaps because a second spring dried up, that they had no choice but to do whatever the owner of the spring demanded of them if they were to survive: here would be a clear case of coercion.[38]

And concerning employment, in a one-industry town or in times of high unemployment, an employer might be able to coerce an employee.[39]

Only in a socialist state would the activities of exchange normally give rise to coercion. In a non-market economy, where the state is the sole provider of services and employment, the state "would possess unlimited powers of coercion."[40] In a socialist state, the state would control the essential data on which an individual bases his actions and a private sphere would not exist (i.e., at least there would be no private property in the means of production), and where no private sphere exists coercion would be more common. In support of his position, Hayek cites Leon Trotsky as saying that opposition to the socialist state will result in starvation.[41]

By broadening the definition of coercion, and limiting its prevention to severe cases, Hayek is able to argue that the normal exchanges that occur in the market are non-coercive and the exchanges that occur in a socialist state are, at least potentially, coercive. We shall briefly analyze Hayek's treatment of coercion and liberty and in doing so we shall present some criticisms that have been directed against his use of these terms.

On two different levels, J. W. N. Watkins argues that Hayek's definition of coercion applies to employer-employee relations, and he criticizes his definition for this reason. Watkins says that Hayek describes coercion as meaning that the coerced becomes a tool of the coercer and that "the only comprehensive design that his actions fit into is that of another mind."[42] Watkins then says,

Again, it seems to me that this view of coercion is too wide. If we consider a worker who performs one simple operation in a complicated technological process which he does not understand, it will be true of him that the "only comprehensive design that his actions fit into is that of another mind."[43]

This would not be a coercive situation according to Hayek's definition. The job of the employee in the above example would at best be a means for his comprehensive design, and his employer may well be as ignorant of his employee's ultimate aims as his employee is ignorant of this complicated process. The employee may even be using his means, which are supplied by his employer in exchange for his labor, for ends which his employer may disapprove of, may be unaware of, or may not understand. By comprehensive design Hayek does not mean the same thing as Watkins. Moreover, if Watkins' example is one of coercion, then it is one of reciprocal coercion, for the employer by being ignorant of his employee's ends would also have to be considered a tool and as fitting into another's comprehensive design. Also, Watkins argues that according to Hayek's definition, "a man who does a job from which he does not want to be sacked and which serves other people's purposes is unfree."[44] This criticism has some merit. If the two conditions of coercion are present (the threat of harm and the intention to change conduct), then the threat of dismissal is a coercive act. However, since Hayek assumes a prosperous economy, and since he virtually identifies a private sphere with a condition of liberty, any criticism of Hayek on these grounds can at best show only a very weak link between coercion and the terms of employment. Rather than too closely associating the terms of employment with coercion, he almost assumes any such relationship out of existence.

In two different essays, Ronald Hamowy criticizes Hayek's example of coercion arising from the ownership of the only spring in an oasis. Hamowy asks, what would be a reasonable or non-coercive price for water? At what price would the sale of the water become coercive? "Is it at one dollar a gallon, ten dollars a gallon, one thousand dollars a gallon?"[45] In his discussion, Hayek says that when a monopolist gains control of an essential product he should be required to charge the same price to each of his customers.[46] Thus, Hamowy's query might be considered a moot one. If Hayek means that whenever an essential commodity comes under monopoly ownership the owner should automatically be required to charge each customer the same price, then the question of what price is coercive is moot because then the price charged is not the criterion by which we apply this sanction, but rather the condition of monopoly and the control of an essential commodity are the criteria by which the sanction is applied.

However, Hamowy certainly does point out that Hayek is not clear on the degree of coercion that becomes a problem. Though Hayek attempts to separate severe coercion from mild coercion, the distinction is not clear. Though he refers to extortion or the "threat of bodily harm to his person or dear ones" as being cases of true coercion, he also says that by "guile and malice" "it is not impossible for a horde of cunning boys to drive an unpopular person out of town."[47] Yet, the second case does not sound as severe as the first. If one attempts to drive a neighbor away by playing loud music, would this be coercion? Would it depend on how loud the music is played? When, if ever, would the state be justified in prohibiting the playing of loud music? Though Hayek intends to distinguish severe coercion from lesser degrees of coercion, he is not entirely clear on this matter.

THE JUSTIFICATION OF COERCION

The state, for Hayek, is a coercive apparatus, though as we shall point out more fully in later chapters it is not solely a coercive apparatus. As a rule, says Hayek, the state is justified in using coercion only to prevent "more severe coercion."[48] However, he believes that it might be better if this criterion applied to the entire legal system rather than to every single rule. This criterion is applied to the entire legal system by delimiting, by rules, a private sphere (which prevents arbitrary interference in our lives by the state and other individuals) so that the data which each individual uses for his ends are kept from the manipulation of others.[49]

Hayek's discussion of a private sphere and the justification of coercion leads him into a brief discourse on John Stuart Mill's *On Liberty,* and especially Mill's distinction between self-regarding and other-regarding actions. Mill believes that there are actions which affect only the voluntary actors (and those who freely associate with them) and actions that affect others. According to Mill, society is justified in regulating actions of only the second type. Hayek quite appropriately notes that most actions will potentially affect others, and he concludes that Mill's distinction "has not proved very useful."[50] However, this criterion, Hayek appears to be saying, is not completely useless and in some cases Mill's criterion is as efficacious as his own. There are some activities that do affect only the voluntary actors and in such cases they should be free to perform these activities. Homosexuality is one instance. It is not that he is opposed to moral rules as such; it is that he does not believe they should be enforced by state power. There may be a case for enforcing moral rules "in public places" but they should not be enforced where only the voluntary actors are involved.[51] Moral rules should exist, but they should not be enforced by anything more than public opinion.[52] Though Hayek finds some limited use for Mill's criterion, he rejects it in favor of his own, which is that coercion can be used only to prevent more severe coercion and he believes that this is most effectively accomplished by rules which delimit protected domains.

Though Hayek offers his own criterion for the use of coercion, I am not certain that he always abides by it. Since the state supplies services other than the prevention of coercion, and since there will never be complete agreement on the extent of state services, he excludes taxation from this rule. He includes violence and fraud with coercion. Also, he allows for coercion according to rules which "secure the best conditions under which the individual may give his activities a coherent, rational pattern," and this use of coercion does not seem to be based on his criterion.[53]

In regard to neighborhood effects, it appears that Hayek's criterion will not apply. For instance, on several different grounds, Hayek does not believe that building regulations infringe the principle of liberty and in fact he regards them as "unquestionably desirable."[54] Yet, the purpose of building regulations is not really to prevent coercion, or even violence, but more broadly to prevent harm—harm to the lives, health, and property of others. Also, attempts to restrict or eliminate the

effects of, say, air pollution by coercive sanctions are undoubtedly based more on the criterion of preventing harm than the
criterion of preventing coercion.

There are some other considerations that lead me to believe
that the criterion that Hayek actually uses to justify coercion
is somewhat broader than the one he actually articulates. In
his criticism of Hayek's example of coercion arising from the
monopoly of water in an oasis, Hamowy says:

Is the owner acting coercively if he refuses to sell his water at any
price: Let us suppose that he looks upon his spring as sacred to his
gods and to offer up its holy water a gross sacrilege. Here is a situation which would not fall under Hayek's definition of coercion, since
the owner of the spring forces no action on the settlers. Yet, it would
appear that, within Hayek's own framework, this is a far worse situation, since the only "choice" left open to the settlers now is dying
of thirst.[55]

Hayek has responded to Hamowy's objections, though he is not
always clear as to which objection he is responding to. In his
response, Hayek compares his example of the oasis to certain
types of emergencies, for example, a situation in which an individual has a heart attack in public and a doctor is on the
scene. In a case of this type, Hayek believes that the potential
savior should have a moral and legal obligation to help even
if he cannot expect any payment in return for his services.[56]
He then goes on to add that any attempt by those rendering
these emergency services to collect more than normal fees for
their services is coercive because it is "a harmful alteration of
the environment."[57] However, by assumption, in Hamowy's
example no one would force any action on any one; those who
could perform the emergency service would simply refuse to
do so under any circumstances. Thus, there is no coercion.
Given the absence of coercion, would Hayek still want those
who are capable of rendering such a service to be legally bound
to do so? Hayek does not precisely answer this question. However, from the context, it appears that he would.[58] If this
interpretation is correct, it follows that Hayek is not justify-
ing coercion on the basis of preventing coercion but on the basis of preventing harm.

Also, Hayek says that there are instances in which "the un-limited control of the owner over his property has to give way," and he refers to this as "good old libertarian doctrine." He then sends his readers to "see David Hume's discussion of the lapse of the rationale of property under the conditions of absolute scarcity in a state of siege."[59] According to Hume, under con-ditions of absolute scarcity one does and should look only to the "motives of necessity and self-preservation."[60] In incorpo-rating this into Hayek's discussion, I can only surmise that he means individuals should not, or at least will not, observe property rights when confronted with a situation like the one Hamowy depicts. In other words, coercion (i.e., threatening the owner with expropriation if he does not sell his water) is jus-tified in order to prevent harm.

Though Hayek states that the justification of coercion is the prevention of more severe coercion, it does not appear that he abides by this criterion in his own applications. He appears to use a broader criterion, that is, the prevention of harm. More-over, some of his statements suggest that the justification of coercion might be even broader than the prevention of harm.[61] However this may be, he does not maintain the criterion that coercion can be used only to prevent more severe coercion, and I am not sure that he can logically maintain this justification.

THE VALUE OF LIBERTY

We shall now turn to the arguments that Hayek advances to justify a state of individual liberty. His argument is in two parts, utilitarian and moral. We shall begin with his utilitar-ian considerations.

Not only does Hayek believe that the individual will best serve himself if he is free, but he also believes that if he is free he will best serve his fellow man. Progress (material and in-tellectual) is a result of freedom, and each of us should want our fellow man to be free if for no other reason than that this will benefit us.[62] Hayek's belief is well summarized by John Stuart Mill's statement that "the only unfailing and perma-nent source of improvement is liberty, since by it there are as many possible independent centers of improvement as there are individuals."[63]

The argument in favor of liberty is largely an epistemological argument. No central authority can ever possess all the knowledge that is possessed separately by a great number of individuals, and to deprive these individuals of the free use of their knowledge is thus to limit the use of this knowledge for the benefit of separate individuals as well as for the public.[64]

Freedom leads to progress because it is an experiment in modes of living. If individuals are free, they will pursue different goals and have different methods of attaining similar goals. By such experimentation, the less successful methods will be driven out of existence by the more successful. As the environment changes different groups will adapt in different ways, and the more successful adaptations will replace the less successful ones.[65] Thus, to inhibit individual freedom is to inhibit experimentation and progress.

Though the importance of intellectual freedom (freedom of research, belief, speech, and discussion) is widely recognized, Hayek believes that the importance of economic freedom, or, more broadly, the freedom of doing things, is not as widely recognized. Not only does Hayek argue that the latter type of freedom is important for material progress, but he argues that it is also important for intellectual progress. He argues that new ideas arise as a result of individuals attempting to cope with changing circumstances. Thus, Hayek concludes that freedom is important even in mundane matters.[66]

By emphasizing the value of individual liberty, Hayek is not denying the value of modern organization. Organization is an extremely powerful tool that human beings can use to achieve their ends. The type of organization that he argues against is the type that is non-voluntary and monopolistic. If there are a number of organizations pursuing a number of goals, and if membership is voluntary, this will aid progress.[67]

Since Hayek has postulated that freedom and progress go hand in hand, one might wonder if this is empirically verifiable. The Soviet Union, for example, seems to have enjoyed progress, and there are few people who will argue that individual liberty is prevalent in that nation. Hayek believes that there has been technological advance in some unfree nations, and he yet believes that a positive relationship between liberty and progress is empirically verifiable. He argues that nations that do not have liberty can usually progress only so far as the free nations do. The unfree nations are able to use the discoveries of the free nations at only a fraction of what it has cost the free nations. They are not discoverers but imitators. If the free nations of the world did not exist, the world would be largely stagnant. For many years, says Hayek, the Soviet Union has been attempting to imitate and live off American technology.[68]

However, there is a way in which progress could take place without freedom. Some technological advances could be brought about more quickly if they "were made the sole aim of humanity."[69] What Hayek means is that if everyone is forced to give up his particular goals and pursue only one goal, that goal would probably be achieved more quickly than otherwise. But here the advance would have to be clearly foreseen, and there would have to be agreement on the achievement of the goal, or else coercion would have to be applied, and other goals, perhaps more valuable after all, would have to be given up.

Freedom, for Hayek, is valuable for its social benefits. However, there is another reason why Hayek values liberty. This reason is a moral reason: human life and human freedom are intrinsically valuable.

In the literature on Hayek, there are several different interpretations of him. Some authors argue that while Hayek values freedom for its social utility, this is merely a secondary reason, and that he primarily values liberty as a moral principle. Others seem to argue that Hayek values liberty only because it leads to material prosperity. Representatives of the first view are Morris M. Wilhelm and Norman P. Barry, and among those expounding the second line of interpretation are Anthony de Crespigny and Christian Bay.[70]

It is the first line of interpretation that is accepted here, and by quoting from Hayek's works we shall attempt to show that liberty and human beings are valued by Hayek for ethical reasons. In *The Road to Serfdom*, Hayek says that individualism is based on "respect for the individual man qua man"[71] and that man derives his dignity "merely from being a man."[72] When he is advocating the rule of law, he says that this implies "the recognition of the inalienable right of the individual, inviolable rights of man."[73] He argues against social planning on the grounds that "the individual would more than ever become a mere means."[74] He says that the individual is not "merely a means to serve the ends of the entity called society or the nation."[75] And, finally, he approvingly quotes Lord Acton as saying that freedom "is not a means to a higher political end. It is itself the highest political end."[76]

In *The Constitution of Liberty,* Hayek argues that "coercion is evil precisely because it thus eliminates an individual as a thinking and valuing person and makes him a bare tool in the achievement of the ends of another."[77] In works published after *The Constitution of Liberty,* he says that freedom is "not merely one value among many but the source of all values."[78] He says that individual liberty is "desirable for itself on ethical grounds."[79] And he says that freedom must be "treated as a supreme principle."[80] "That freedom is the matrix required for the growth of moral values," writes Hayek, "is almost self-evident." He adds, "it is only where the individual has choice, and its inherent responsibility, that he has occasion to affirm existing values, to contribute to their further growth, and to earn moral merit."[81] Though some authors argue that Hayek values individual freedom only because it leads to material prosperity, the evidence just cited does not seem to support this view.

CONCLUSION

Hayek believes that liberty is compatible with other values and even that it is necessary for the growth of other values. His emphasis is on the importance, indeed the precedence, of liberty in regard to other goals. And it is in regard to this emphasis on the priority of freedom that Hayek is distinguished from many other contemporary philosophers. Some will argue that freedom can be curtailed in order to secure more material equality or to secure more participation in government. Hayek does not.

Freedom is the central aspect of Hayek's political philosophy. And it is to Hayek's analysis of how to preserve liberty that we now turn.

NOTES

1. The argument for liberty does not completely apply to those, e.g., children, who are unable to care for themselves. See Hayek, 1960a, pp. 76–77.

2. Hayek, 1960a, p. 421 n. 1.

3. Hayek, 1960a, pp. 12, 21.

4. Hayek, 1960a, p. 11. In the same work, p. 12, Hayek also describes liberty as independence from the arbitrary will of another. In Hayek, 1971b, p. 29, he describes a state of freedom as one "in which each can use his knowledge for his own purposes. . . ."

5. Hayek, 1960a, p. 133.

6. Hayek, 1960a, pp. 12–13.

7. Hayek, 1960a, pp. 16–17.

8. Cranston, 1967, p. 26.

9. Hayek, 1960a, pp. 9, 421 n. 2.

10. Hayek, 1960a, p. 12. Also, Hayek, 1967b, p. 348.

11. This line of interpretation is suggested in Plato, 1960, esp. pp. 49–52, where Socrates argues that even if one can always do as one wants, one is not necessarily powerful. Also, see the discussion of virtue and the soul in Plato, 1945, pp. 129–144.

12. Hayek, 1960a, p. 15.

13. See Hayek, 1960a, p. 138.

14. Hayek, 1960a, p. 15.

15. Rousseau, 1950, pp. 94, 19.

16. Hayek, 1960a, pp. 13–14.

17. See Berlin, 1970, pp. xliii, 121, 122, 129, 130, 166. Also see Hayek, 1978c, p. 143.

18. Hayek, 1960a, p. 423 n. 14, and p. 425 n. 26.

19. Hayek, 1960a, p. 17.

20. Hayek, 1960a, pp. 16, 18.

21. Hayek, 1960a, p. 17.

22. Hayek, 1960a, p. 18. Wooton, 1945, p. 11, also says that material well-being and freedom should not be confused. "Prisoners would not become free men even if they were looked after as well as race horses."

23. Hayek, 1960a, p. 17.

24. Hayek, 1960a, pp. 134–135, 449–450 n. 4. Also see Hayek, 1979, p. 80.

25. Lasswell and Kaplan, 1950, p. 75.

26. Lasswell and Kaplan, 1950, p. 75.

27. Russell, 1938, p. 35.

28. Hayek, 1960a, p. 134. On p. 133, Hayek argues that coercion implies that the coerced still chooses though among the least painful alternatives that have been thrust upon him by the coercer.

29. Hayek, 1960a, p. 133. Also see pp. 13, 20, 21, 135, 144.

30. Hayek, 1960a, pp. 143–144.

31. Hayek, 1960a, pp. 134, 139.

32. Hayek, 1960a, p. 140.

33. Hayek, 1960a, pp. 138–139.

34. Hayek, 1960a, p. 137.

35. Hayek, 1960a, pp. 138, 146.

36. Hayek, 1960a, p. 136.

37. Hayek, 1960a, p. 136.

38. Hayek, 1960a, p. 136.

39. Hayek, 1960a, pp. 136–137. Also see Hayek, 1980, p. 41.

40. Hayek, 1960a, p. 139.

41. Hayek, 1960a, p. 137.

42. Watkins, 1961, p. 43. Also see Hayek, 1960a, p. 134.

43. Watkins, 1961, p. 43.

44. Watkins, 1961, pp. 42–43.

45. Hamowy, 1961, p. 29. Also see Hamowy, 1971, pp. 354–355.

46. Hayek, 1960a, p. 137. For a criticism of his view, see Barry, 1979, p. 73. In Hayek, 1979, pp. 84–85, Hayek reformulates his position. However, his reformulation will not obviate Barry's criticism.

47. Hayek, 1960a, p. 138.

48. Hayek, 1960a, p. 144.

49. Hayek, 1960a, pp. 144–145.

50. Hayek, 1960a, p. 45. Mill, 1956, p. 13, justifies coercion on the basis of preventing harm to others.

51. Hayek, 1960a, pp. 145, 451 n. 18.

52. Mill, 1956, p. 7, would probably regard such an expression of public opinion as an infringement of liberty. In this respect, Hayek believes that Mill "overstated the case for liberty." Hayek, 1960a, p. 146.

53. Hayek, 1960a, pp. 143–144.

54. Hayek, 1960a, pp. 354–355.

55. Hamowy, 1961, p. 29; Hamowy, 1971, p. 356.

56. Hayek, 1967b, p. 350.

57. Hayek, 1967b, p. 350.

58. Also see Hayek, 1976e, p. 36.

59. Hayek, 1967b, p. 350.

60. Hume, 1972, p. 187.

61. See above, p. 21.

62. See Hayek, 1960a, ch. 2, esp. p. 32.

63. Mill, 1956, p. 86.

64. See Hayek, 1948, chs. 2, 4; Hayek, 1978c, ch. 14; Hayek, 1960a, chs. 2, 3.

65. Hayek, 1960a, p. 85.

66. Hayek, 1960a, pp. 33–34.

67. Hayek, 1960a, p. 37.

68. Hayek, 1960a, p. 47.

69. Hayek, 1944, p. 53.

70. Wilhelm, 1972, p. 172; Barry, 1979, p. 67; de Crespigny, 1975, p. 58; Bay, 1971, pp. 94, 124.

71. Hayek, 1944, pp. 14, 214.

72. Hayek, 1944, p. 141.

73. Hayek, 1944, p. 84.

74. Hayek, 1944, p. 96.

75. Hayek, 1944, p. 149.

76. Hayek, 1944, p. 70.

77. Hayek, 1960a, p. 21.

78. Hayek, 1967b, p. 230.

79. Hayek, 1976e, p. 71.

80. Hayek, 1971b, p. 71.

81. Hayek, 1967b, p. 230.

III.

Economic Order and Freedom

Hayek's view of the most appropriate economic arrangements conducive to freedom is intimately connected with his view of law. However, since he has written so extensively on the subject of law, his treatment of this topic will be considered separately in the next chapter, and in this chapter we shall present only those considerations of his legal philosophy that are essential to an understanding of his economic doctrines. There is one other area of Hayek's thought that is essential to understanding both his economic doctrines and his legal philosophy. This is his view of society. Since his understanding of society is logically prior to either his economic doctrines or his legal philosophy, our analysis will begin with a presentation of his view of society.

SOCIETY

In his discussion, Hayek remarks that social life is possible only when there is order, that is, only when there is coordination among the activities of individuals. He alternately refers to this coordination of activities (or order) by the words pattern, system, and structure.[1]

There are, says Hayek, two types of social order and each one has a distinct origin. The most commonly recognized type of order is one that is imposed by an act of human will. It is designed and created for a purpose, and it is an exogenous, created, or artificial order. In contrast, the second type of order arises from within, for example, by individuals adjusting their actions to the actions of each other, and it is an endogenous, evolutionary, spontaneous, or self-generating order. For brevity, as well as to keep a distinction between the orders, Hayek uses the Greek words *taxis* to refer to a created order and *cosmos* to refer to an evolutionary order.

According to Hayek, society is a form of cosmos. Like language, law, and morals, it is the result of an evolutionary process rather than the result of human design. "Man acted before he thought. . . ."[2] As man acts, he gradually builds up a system of rules of conduct. These rules of conduct are abstract; they limit an individual's range of actions but do not prescribe a particular action. Circumscribed by rules that only prohibit certain types of activities, an individual is free to use his knowledge for his own purposes. Thus, society has no purpose per se but merely the function of allowing an individual to pursue a goal.

Since each individual is confronted by a number of particular facts which are unknown to any one other individual (or group of individuals), this order can be extremely complex. The order can be complex because it takes account of millions of facts that, though unknown in entirety by any one entity, are known by someone. As each individual adjusts his behavior to the constantly changing facts of his environment, the entire structure of human relationships adapts to these changes.

Society is an abstract order in which individuals are related to each other on the basis of rules (which are the same for all, or at least for large segments of the population) and particular facts.[3] It is unlike both an organization (which is arranged hierarchically) and a biological organism (an order in which individual elements cannot change places). As long as a certain pattern of relationships is maintained, individual elements can change places, and the number of elements can change, and the order will continue to function. By changing the rules, we may change a particular individual's place in the social order, but since his place is also determined by innumerable facts, we shall never know beforehand how the change of rules will affect a particular individual.

In the realm of social order, an organization is a type of taxis. In contrast to a cosmos or society, an organization is a deliberately contrived structure and it is created to achieve a purpose, for example, to make and sell a product. Since an organization has an end, its rules are concrete rather than abstract (or at least less abstract than the rules of a cosmos). The rules are concrete in the sense that they arrange individuals into a hierarchical pattern and give each individual a particular task so that the goals of the organization can be achieved. Unlike a cosmos, an organization is directed by a single mind. Thus, it is a relatively simple order that is incapable of ascertaining all of the constantly changing facts that affect human life. An organization is one of many components of society and it can achieve its purpose only because the information it needs (e.g., information concerning the relative values of goods and services that it uses) is supplied as a result of the interactions of many individuals and organizations in a spontaneous order.

Though Hayek believes that there are two types of order, he says that the distinction between them is often blurred, and he attributes this confusion to two sources.

First, there is a misleading distinction, which he traces back as far as the ancient Greeks, between phenomena which are natural and phenomena which are artificial.[4] In discussing phenomena, the Greeks used the words *physei, nomō,* and *thesei;* best translated as natural, conventional, and deliberately created. The confusion centers around the conventional. Since the conventional is not a deliberate human construction, some individuals came to refer to it as natural. Though more prevalently, others thought that since it is the result of human action, it must, like the deliberately constructed, be artificial. The failure to appreciate the distinction between different types of artificial phenomena has lead to the conclusion that everything that is the result of human action is a designed construction, including human society.

The second source of confusion emanates from the different functions of government. Though a cosmos and a taxis operate on distinct sets of rules, government uses both types of rules. Since the survival of society depends on the observance of abstract rules, government will have to enforce at least some of these rules. However, for the purposes of enforcing these rules as well as to supply goods and services that the market cannot supply, the government will have to operate according to the concrete rules of a taxis and assign particular tasks to particular government employees. Since a single organization (government) uses two types of rules, the distinction between these rules and the resulting orders has been obscured.[5]

As we pointed out in the first chapter, Hayek divides political theorists into two categories: evolutionary rationalists and constructivist rationalists. The former correctly view society as an undesigned process rather than as an entity. Constructivist rationalists, on the other hand, are inclined to ascribe characteristics to society, for example, that it thinks or acts, or is just or unjust, that could not possibly apply to a process, though they can and do apply to individuals and organizations. Unlike the evolutionary rationalists, the constructivist rationalists either do not perceive the distinction between a self-generating order and a deliberately created order, or else they believe that a deliberately created order is always superior to a self-generating order.

If the distinction between a taxis and a cosmos is not maintained, Hayek believes that an abstract pattern of activities will be replaced by the more easily recognizable pattern of an organization. Rules of organization are an effective means of coordinating human activities only when the number of purposes and the number of facts are relatively limited. As organizations become more complex, even they, to a degree, use abstract rules. If the leader of an organization wants to benefit from knowledge that he does not possess, he will merely determine the task to be achieved, for example, and allow his subordinate to determine the method. However, society is an extremely complicated pattern of activities that takes account of the diverse purposes of many individuals and makes use of information that cannot be ascertained by any one entity.[6] This order cannot be improved, but rather will be distorted, by mixing organizational directives with abstract rules because the directives will refer to only particular aspects of an interrelated system of actions. By revising the rules on which the order rests, it is possible to improve the order, but it cannot be improved by the method of specific directions.[7] If rules of organization replace abstract rules, the information that is dispersed among millions of people will no longer be taken into account in our actions, and our advanced civilization, which is based on the use of this knowledge, will decay.

Moreover, if society is turned into an organization, individual liberty will cease to exist. A purposeless and abstract order will be replaced by an order in which common ends are imposed on everyone and individuals are arranged into a hierarchy in order to achieve these ends.

SOCIALISM

This brings to a conclusion our presentation of Hayek's considerations on society. The relationship between society and the economic order can probably be perceived already. Just as society is a series of mutually adjusting activities between individuals so is the market. The term cosmos can be used to describe both phenomena. The market is a process, a very complicated process, through which many facts are taken into account. Socialism, which has been proposed by some to replace the market, is an organization, or taxis, which cannot take account of all the facts which the market can. According to Hayek, socialism is not conducive to either economic efficiency or freedom. Our examination of the economic arrangements that Hayek believes are conducive, or not conducive, to liberty will begin with his critique of socialism. Two terms in Hayek's vocabulary are extremely important for understanding his economic doctrines: knowledge (or information) and agreement.[8] The term agreement is most important to an understanding of why freedom and socialism are incompatible. The term knowledge is essential in understanding why socialism is inefficient. After determining what Hayek means by socialism, we shall, in turn, address Hayek's reasons for regarding socialism as inefficient and as illiberal.

Unlike a system of private enterprise, socialism means that all productive resources are owned and directed by a single public entity. It is a method rather than an end. Though all socialists desire to organize the means of production to achieve a goal (e.g., material equality), not all socialists have the same purpose in mind, and the monopoly ownership of the means of production can be used, for example, to increase material inequality.[9] In essence, socialism specifies that economic decisions are to be made by one entity. It does not say what the decisions are.

Socialism is a method of allocating resources. What, economically speaking, is the problem with having these resources allocated by a single entity?

The problem, in principle, is knowledge, or more correctly, a lack of knowledge, and also the communication, and especially the rapid communication, of knowledge (or information). Moreover, a problem arises because there is a limited amount of resources which have a potentially unlimited number of uses.[10] Under socialism, someone, we shall say the government, must not only find a use for these resources but must find the most efficient use for these resources.

The government, in order to solve this problem, will have to have an amount of knowledge and a type of knowledge that it cannot have. Before the government starts dividing up the resources among various ends, it will first have to know what these ends are. Thus, the government will have to have an amount of information that is equal to that possessed by each individual. At any point in time, each individual will probably have a series of preferences. The government will have to know what these preferences are and will have to know the relative value of each of the preferences. Once the government knows the ends at which it is aiming, it will have to decide the best way to provide for these ends. It will have to decide what resources to use in the production of each good and it will have to decide on the combination of resources to be used in the production of each good. How will the government come to know all individual preferences and how will it come to know the kind, amount, and combination of resources that will most efficiently satisfy these preferences?

According to Hayek, we know what preferences are only as a result of the market. We know what resources, the kind, amount, and combination, are most efficient in producing goods only as a result of the market.[11] Once we prohibit the market from functioning we no longer know. To assume that you can create a rational economic order is to assume that you know a priori the outcome of the economic process. It is only by allowing this process to function that we can ascertain preferences and satisfy these preferences efficiently.

Even if we assumed that at any particular point in time we did know all preferences, and the most efficient way to provide for them, this would be of only the most ephemeral benefit to us. If just one fact changes this could have far-reaching effects. Suppose preferences change. How will it be determined what they are? What changes will this necessitate in the use of each of the resources needed to satisfy this new series of preferences? Suppose copper becomes more scarce. How should it now be allocated? What effect will this have on the use of tin or brass, or any of the products these resources comprise? Suppose the weather changes. What effect will this have on agricultural products? Will the effect on agricultural products have an effect on preferences? If so, how much? Will any effect on agricultural products have an effect in any other areas of the economy? If so, where? How much? Suppose, as Hayek does, that many different facts change and change often: how well will the government be able to respond?[12]

Socialism is a centrally directed economic system. The market functions as well as it does because it is a decentralized system. For the most efficient allocation of resources, people continually have to adjust their behavior to a large number of continuously changing facts. Often, these facts are known only to certain individuals. "Particular circumstances of time and place" might give rise to "unique information."[13] Individuals will be able to respond to these facts, and respond rapidly, only if they are free to take advantage of them. The problem is one of knowledge and the communication of knowledge. To assume that one source can direct the economic activities of each and every individual is to assume that this source knows all the information that is dispersed among millions of people.[14] It is further to assume that this knowledge can be conveyed to a central authority and that this central authority can then convey all this information back to all these individuals in the form of telling them what they ought to do.

To help bring out the difference between socialism and the market, we shall briefly focus on Hayek's analysis of the market. The market is a decentralized system in which everyone is able to act on unique information. No one has complete knowledge of all the information upon which an efficient allocation of resources depends. How then does the market tend toward an efficient allocation of resources? It is because of the "marvel" of prices.[15]

Essentially, the price system is a communications system. If a particular resource becomes more scarce, this will be reflected in its price, and it will affect the prices of the products that contain it, the prices of substitute goods, the prices of complementary goods, and so on. With perhaps only a few people actually knowing of the original source of the scarcity, individuals will use less of this resource. Thus, prices convey information that cause individuals to coordinate their separate actions and this coordination takes place without anyone issuing an order.[16] The information that is contained in, and rapidly transmitted by, prices is absent in a centrally directed economic system.

One might more or less accept what Hayek has to say on the role of prices and the inability of central direction to effectively replace the market and yet disagree with him. The reason might be that theoretically socialism has advanced beyond the stage of central direction to that of competition. Oskar Lange has written an essay in which he attempts to show how competition can be combined with socialism. Lange envisions a semi-competitive socialist state in which a market is retained for wages and consumer goods. All the other prices for the factors of production are determined by a central authority as a result of a method of trial and error, which he argues is not that much different than the way prices are determined in a free market.[17] It may be thought that Hayek cannot apply his criticisms to the type of system envisioned by Lange because Lange's system is organized competitively and designed to preserve the price mechanism. However, Hayek advances arguments that are consistent with his criticisms of centralized socialism. First, since the means of production will be socialized, all new investment will still have to be determined by a central authority. Also, Hayek argues that under Lange's system prices for capital goods will have to be fixed and changed by authorities, and since a great number of items will have to be valued, prices will be standardized and will not reflect differences of place and quality. Therefore, prices will not convey as much information as true market prices and this information will not be conveyed as quickly as it is in a system of private enterprise. Moreover, Lange's trial and error method of valuing capital goods may be effective if prices are stable but in the real world where the prices of the factors of production are all constantly changing it will not be effective, and in regard to non-standardized goods and services the method of trial and error cannot work.[18]

Hayek does not say a solution to the problem of an efficient allocation of resources in a socialist state will never be found, though he thinks such a discovery highly unlikely.[19] It seems, however, that if ever a solution is found it will have to be on a basis of competition.[20] If, in the absence of private property, a market order is possible, competition will have to be between firms and not merely industries.[21] And he thinks that, in achieving this socialist state, planning will probably have to be given up so that prices can function. If the purpose of socialism is redistributive, this type of competitive socialism will be restricted in its ability to achieve its specific aims. And if, as Hayek quotes one socialist as saying, the aim is to overthrow competition, then the socialists have surely not achieved anything they have attempted.[22]

Though Hayek does not rule out the possibility of an efficient allocation of resources under socialism, he does believe, unless there is new information, that the efficiency argument against socialism is a closed affair to the detriment of socialism. In fact, he says: "Surely it is high time for us to cry from the house-tops that the intellectual foundations of socialism have all collapsed."[23]

Though Hayek feels that the intellectual foundations for socialism have collapsed, it is interesting to note that there are other highly regarded non-socialist economists who do not share this attitude. The late Joseph A. Schumpeter believed that the problem of economic calculation could be solved in a socialist state.[24] Hayek, however, comments upon and disagrees with Schumpeter's analysis. Briefly, the controversy between Schumpeter and Hayek traces back at least as far as the publication, originally in 1920, of an article by Ludwig von Mises. In this article, von Mises argues that socialism will be inefficient because there is no market for productive goods. Hence, there will be no prices for the factors of production, and hence there can be no rational calculation of cost.[25] In what is apparently a denial of von Mises' thesis, Schumpeter asserts "that consumers in evaluating ('demanding') consumers' goods ipso facto also evaluate the means of production which enter into the production of those goods."[26] Hayek cites and criticizes this remark by Professor Schumpeter. Hayek says, "it is evident, however, that the values of the factors of production do not depend solely on the valuation of the consumers' goods but also on the conditions of supply of the various factors of production."[27]

Also, Henry C. Wallich believes that a centrally directed economy is not necessarily less productive than the free market. He says,

our own experience confirms it. We need recall only what the nation did during two world wars. When maximum output was needed, we shifted to centralized control and direction. When the emergency was over, the shift was reversed—fortunately. The lesson is plain. A free economy can perform very well, as ours has. It can provide a rapidly rising standard of output and consumption. But if absolute maximum of output and growth is wanted there are other methods.[28]

The war years seem to offer an example to some that planning can be as productive as the free market, and it also offers an example to others that planning (though not necessarily socialism) may be compatible with individual liberty.[29] Since this example seems to challenge the principle behind Hayek's criticism, we shall briefly consider it.

As we have shown, Hayek begins his criticism with the premise that there are limited resources and a multiplicity of ends. The problem is to discover and to satisfy these ends. At least implicitly, the example of wartime experience denies the premise. There is no longer a multiplicity of ends but a single (or at least a dominating) end—winning the war. Hayek would argue that during war a predominant end does exist and he would argue that this end will best be achieved by organizing the population.[30] He would also argue that this is anomalous and that normally there are a number of competing ends and that therefore socialism will be inefficient.

We shall now take up Hayek's criticism of socialism on the basis of its alleged illiberal status. However, before proceeding to an analysis of freedom under socialism, there is one point that must be clarified. Hayek believes socialism will destroy individual freedom. He writes that socialism is a species of collectivism and in so doing he associates socialism with nazism, fascism, and communism.[31] Nazism, fascism, and (though probably to a lesser extent) communism are recognized as evil. By denying the possibility of individual freedom under socialism, and associating it with these doctrines, Hayek is not casting aspersions on the character of socialists. He is not saying that socialists are immoral, but rather that socialists are highly idealistic men and women who are guilty of intellectual error. In fact, Hayek says that in his youth he was a socialist. His socialist views led him to study economics and only by this study was he able to ascertain that he was mistaken in his belief that socialism would achieve the ends he sought. In the following paragraphs, it should not be thought that Hayek is arguing that socialists want to destroy liberty but rather that unwittingly they may do so.[32]

If socialism replaces the market, it means that a system of decentralized individual planning will be replaced by a system of centralized planning. The question is not, Should there be planning? The question is, Who should plan?[33]

As we saw in the efficiency argument, there are numerous ends and limited resources. These considerations not only have important economic consequences, but they have important philosophical consequences as well. If there are many ends and limited resources with which to satisfy these ends, someone must decide which are to be satisfied and which are not. And among the ends to be satisfied, someone must decide the priorities. If the decision on ends is to be made by a central

authority for everyone, it must be assumed, at least if freedom is to be preserved, that everyone agrees on the ends to be
achieved.

If agreement is absent, freedom is impossible because it
means that someone is choosing goals for another. The purpose of planning is to achieve something. If individual planning is replaced by central planning, it means that there is
one plan that each and every individual is attempting to
achieve. Agreement thus becomes of paramount importance.
If one does not agree with the goals, one must nevertheless
strive for the goals. If one must seek to achieve something that
one not only may not want, but may be opposed to, one is not
free.[34]

Central economic planning is only as popular as it is because each of the advocates of planning assumes either that
he will be doing the planning or that the planning authority
will adopt his scale of values. Each of us have a hierarchy of
values which we believe to be perfectly reasonable and we believe that if only we were given the chance to explain our values to other individuals, they would adopt our values.[35] What
we find difficult to believe is that others will disagree with us.

Hayek worries that a unitary plan will be implemented and
that freedom will thereby be lost. But he fears more than just
this. If agreement on ends does not exist, force or propaganda
may be necessary, either to compel people to achieve goals they
do not want, or, to convince them that the goals of the central
authority are identical with their own.[36]

Besides a lack of agreement on ends, there are other reasons that lead Hayek to doubt the possibility of individual liberty in a socialist state. These other reasons are based more
on a consideration of means rather than ends.

For Hayek, there are only two ways individual economic acts
can be adjusted to each other. The first is via the impersonal
process of the market, by which individuals adjust their own
activities to the activities of others, and the second is by central direction, by which the government adjusts the activities
of each and every individual to one another.[37]

In the market, individuals adjust their activities in regard
to prices and wages. Resources, including labor, are allocated

by an impersonal system of prices and wages. From Hayek's efficiency argument, we have seen that prices (and wages) can be determined only through the market. No one can ascertain prices and wages without a functioning system. Individuals are able to adjust their separate actions to one another because prices and wages indicate what they should do to best serve themselves as well as others. But where there is no market, there is no impersonal system of prices and wages that can effectively allocate resources.

If the market does not function, prices and wages cannot indicate how individuals should act. This leads Hayek to the conclusion that there will be, indeed there can be, no freedom of occupation. If wages now serve to tell people how they should employ their labor, the absence of the market means that another method will have to be used to direct human labor. This other method will be human direction.[38] Hayek is trying to make the point that in order to fulfill successfully a comprehensive economic plan the government will have to do more than merely determine the use of inanimate productive resources, it also will have to determine the uses of human resources. Though in a market society everyone's fate will depend on ability and luck, in a socialist state individuals will occupy certain positions as a result of the decisions of political authorities.[39]

Many people, believes Hayek, support socialism because its harmful effects, if any, will not be crucial. Socialism concerns merely economics and not such important things as civil and political liberties. Hayek tries to show that this is not true. He argues that if one source controls all the means it necessarily controls the ends.[40] As we have just seen, Hayek believes that for a socialist state to be successful it will have to control human resources as well as natural resources. He further argues that some of our most precious political liberties will be threatened by socialism. In particular, he argues that socialism will threaten freedom of expression.

Hayek does not understand, for instance, "how the freedom of the press is to be safeguarded when the supply of paper and all the channels of distribution are controlled by the planning authority."[41] In a system of private enterprise, economic resources can be used to achieve ends of which the government disapproves. However, in a society in which one entity owns all the means of production, and where this entity is committed to achieving particular goals, "can there be much doubt that this power would be used for the ends of which the authority approves and to prevent the pursuits of ends which it disapproves?"[42] In the socialist state there is only one source that can satisfy our wishes, and this source is committed to the pursuit of a unitary plan. Rather than the state satisfying our desires, we shall be a means to satisfy the desires of the state.

Another prominent free market economist, Milton Friedman, argues in the same vein. In a section of his book where he is discussing the advocacy of "unpopular causes," he says that in a free market "the suppliers of paper are as willing to sell it to the *Daily Worker* as to the *Wall Street Journal*." He wonders if a government that controls all resources will supply individuals with the means that might eventually cause its own downfall. He speculates that if a socialist government desires to preserve freedom of expression, "it could establish a bureau for subsidizing subversive propaganda."[43] But Friedman, like Hayek, believes the government will be more interested in securing its preservation than in undermining it.

For the reasons presented, Hayek believes "that socialism is bound to become totalitarian."[44] As will be shown shortly, he also believes that attempts at a mixed economy could lead to the same condition. Many commentators, like the well-known economist Robert L. Heilbroner, suggest that Hayek's arguments on this subject contain many "exaggerations."[45] It seems that Arnold Brecht criticizes Hayek's thesis on the same grounds.

The question of compatibility of democracy and socialism, therefore, is still an open one. There is good reason to believe that it is not necessary to go all the way along the totalitarian road if a majority should be bent on carrying through socialism, although certain modifications in the process of economic legislation and administration will be necessary.[46]

There is reason, though, to believe that Hayek does not exaggerate the dangers of socialism. We shall examine Hayek's thesis on the basis of a consideration that he does not discuss.

The consideration to be examined is suggested by Robert Nozick's discussion of socialism and distributive justice, though our particular example and application of it will differ from his.[47] Nozick tends to believe that if we have a socialist state we cannot keep it socialist without forbidding all voluntary exchange. Our example runs as follows. We have an economic system in which the government owns and directs all productive goods. An individual desires to earn his living by writing political commentaries. For whatever reason, he cannot or does not procure a position with the government in this capacity. He therefore saves the money he earns from his employment with the state and begins purchasing writing materials. In his private hours, he writes and distributes, at a price, political commentaries. His venture is successful. He soon quits his job with the government and works on his political journal full time. He is doing so well that he hires other employees, for example, other writers, and people to sell and deliver the journal. This possible scenario is outside the limits of socialism. If other people see how successful he is, they may attempt to do the same thing in different fields. Unless the socialist government prohibits this sort of activity, it may find out that it is no longer socialist. Voluntary action may destroy the government. If the government forbids this sort of activity, it is obvious that it is prohibiting economic freedom on the part of both the producer and the consumer. In the case of our particular example, if the government prohibits this individual from writing, hiring, and distributing, it is abridging his freedom of expression. Yet, if the state is to maintain the sole ownership and the sole direction of the means of production, this individual must be prevented from writing and distributing his political commentaries.[48]

There is reason to believe that Hayek does not exaggerate. All voluntary action that could possibly be construed as economic may have to be prevented. There appear to be only three ways that such action can be prevented. The first is that everyone is so wealthy that no economic transactions would go on outside the state. The second is that everyone is so poor and so busy procuring their survival within the socialist state that no one would have the means to engage in any other activity. The third is by prohibition.

INTERVENTIONISM

Among other criticisms leveled at Hayek's analysis of the effect of socialism on individual liberty is that Hayek examines only one form of planning, and that this is the least attractive form of planning. Perhaps among the most famous of political observers to make such an argument is R. H. Tawney.[49] In effect, Tawney argues that even if we concede to Hayek that if the government owns and directs all resources freedom will be threatened, we do not have to conclude that freedom and socialism are incompatible. The socialist government does not need to own everything. The government merely needs to direct the flow of capital, and it need only own the major industries. Under such circumstances, the government could sell certain items at a loss instead of a profit. Presumably, this will have the economically beneficial effect of allowing people to procure certain goods more easily than before. Politically, since the government will not own all resources, this will remove any potential danger of totalitarianism.

Hayek, however, does deal with such considerations. In recent years, Hayek treats such arguments in a more serious manner than he does socialism. Hayek believes that socialism as a comprehensive philosophy is "dead."[50] The chief danger to freedom does not come from socialists but from interventionists.

The type of argument that Tawney espouses seems to convey the thought that if a full-fledged socialism will destroy individual liberty, a judicious mixture of socialism with the free market will not. Hayek does not believe that a mixed economy will indefinitely preserve individual liberty.

Though as a philosophy socialism may have perished, some of the measures taken under the name of the welfare state could ultimately lead to socialism. Hayek says that the term *welfare state* does not have a clear meaning, but that it does indicate that government concerns itself with problems other than the prevention of violence, for example, caring for people who cannot care for themselves. Hayek has no objection to using the apparatus of government to alleviate poverty, but he does find some of the methods of government aid objectionable.

For instance, when government enters a particular field it

often claims a monopoly privilege and effectively prevents others from entering the field. One example Hayek gives is social security. Though it may be appropriate, because of "third-party risks," to require everyone to purchase old age insurance, it is an unnecessary infringement of freedom to require everyone to purchase this insurance from one source.[51]

Moreover, some attempts by government to deal with poverty related matters involve government intervention in the market to control prices, and this Hayek regards as pernicious. As an example of government intervention, Hayek mentions rent control. He finds rent control to be self-defeating. If rents are high because there is a housing shortage, any attempt to enforce a price ceiling that is less than market value will discourage investment and perpetuate the shortage.[52] However, Hayek does not oppose government intervention on the basis of its efficiency or inefficiency in particular cases, but rather, on principle, he opposes all attempts at combining a command economy with a market order.

For three closely related reasons, Hayek believes that any attempt to control individual prices will lead us closer to socialism. Since prices convey information and coordinate individual activities, an attempt to control the price of a particular commodity will cause a distortion in the economic order and the only way this distortion can be remedied is by either a return to market pricing or for the government to control an ever increasing number of prices. In the case of rent control, if the ceiling on rent is set below the market price, a shortage will develop. In order to ensure that supply will match demand, the government can do one of two things: drop the controls or attempt to control the prices of construction and maintenance, for example.

Second, Hayek fears that intervention will destroy liberty because the beneficial effects of intervention are easily perceived, and the harmful effects of intervention are anything but easily perceived. Intervention is a more or less solitary act of coercion that is intended to produce a particular result. The acceptance of freedom in the market is not based upon the consideration that it will produce any particular result, only that on the whole it will produce a more desirable order than will central direction. Turning to the example of rent control, the immediate effect of intervention will be good, at least for renters, because the price of housing will be lower than the market price. However, the shortage of housing which rent control will cause will not appear simultaneously with its imposition, and it may appear only after such a length of time that the price control will not be recognized as the cause of the shortage. Thus, the harmful effects of intervention may not be noticed. If we make our judgment on intervention versus freedom on a case by case method, the unknown effects of freedom will perhaps always be forsaken for the known effects of intervention.[53]

Last, Hayek believes that all acts of intervention must be ruled out in principle or else there will be no mechanism by which we can prevent a series of acts of intervention that in their totality may destroy a market order.[54]

Hayek does discuss less extreme methods of government economic control than the complete ownership of the means of production, and he criticizes them on the basis of principle. By basing his argument against interventionism on principle rather than on the prudential considerations of a case by case method, he appears to be dogmatic. This, however, is not unintentional. It is only, believes Hayek, by a strict application of principles that makes no exceptions for expediency that freedom will be able to survive in the long run.[55] In fact, the greatest threat to freedom today does not come from doctrinaire socialists but rather from the practical minded who wish to dispense with all principles and add up the pluses and minuses of each discrete act of government intervention.[56] The non-ideologues do not realize that the market is a complicated order and that attempts to correct the market by intervention will instead gradually destroy the market and individual freedom. Though there may be few who intentionally want to create a socialist state, as the market continues to wither under government intervention, we may "still establish it, albeit unintentionally."[57]

SOCIAL JUSTICE

There is a special type of intervention, based on the ideals of socialism, that Hayek believes is very popular and for that reason especially dangerous. He refers to it as social, or distributive, justice. In recent years, no topic has occupied Hayek's time more than social justice. Since Hayek has spent much time analyzing social justice, we shall here treat it separately from his general statement on intervention.

The basic consideration behind social justice is that society should treat individuals justly and thus that there should be a morally meaningful pattern of distributing wealth among the members of society. However, among proponents of the concept, it might be debated whether that pattern of distribution should be based on, for example, need, merit, or equality. Unlike earlier socialist schemes in which a just pattern of distribution would result from the governmental ownership of the means of production, the contemporary quest for social justice attempts to achieve a just distribution of income within the market by taxation, government services, and the fixing of prices and wages. Despite the popularity and widespread acceptance of social justice, Hayek argues that the term is meaningless, that a patterned distribution is unjust, and that attempts to achieve social justice will progressively lead us closer to totalitarianism.[58]

At the very least, the first of Hayek's criticisms is based on deductions from his definitions of justice and society. According to Hayek, the term justice can only be meaningfully applied to the conduct of individuals and it cannot apply to a state of affairs that has not been brought about by a thinking and acting being or entity. A person can be treated either justly or unjustly by, for example, the government, or a corporation, or another person. A particular state of affairs, in and of itself, cannot be said to be just or unjust merely because it is desirable or undesirable. If someone is ill, this is unfortunate, though it is not unjust unless someone is responsible for causing the illness.[59]

Society is merely a process and it is not a thinking and acting entity that distributes wealth. In the cosmos of the market, the interactions of a number of people determine wages and prices. There is no one person or group that decides what wages will be. If someone did determine wages and prices, one could ask for justice from him. But where no one has determined wages and prices, "who is supposed to have been unjust?"[60]

Hayek believes that the term *right* is being misused. As an example, he points to the *Universal Declaration of Human Rights* of the United Nations which stipulates, among other things, that people as members of society are by right to be provided with periodic holidays with pay and to share in scientific advances and the benefits of those advances. Yet, if someone has a right to something, someone else must have an obligation to provide it.[61] Social justice and the new social and economic rights "are based on the interpretation of society as a deliberately made organization by which everybody is employed."[62] In a market society, these rights are meaningless because there is no one who is under the obligation to provide them. In order to make these rights effective, society must be turned from a process into an all-embracing organization, because only where someone is responsible for a state of affairs can another have rights.

Besides arguing that the concept of social justice is meaningless in a market order, Hayek says that attempts to achieve social justice are in fact unjust, immoral, and impossible of attainment. If one seeks to achieve social justice within the market, only some people can be accorded the benefits of a nonmarket determined salary. This is a privilege that cannot be extended to all in a functioning market. Thus, the government will have to treat some people differently than others. This is unjust. If one seeks social justice by turning a cosmos into a comprehensive taxis, individuals will be prevented from using their knowledge for their ends and they will have to relinquish moral responsibility for their actions to a directing mind. This is immoral. Moreover, even if a process is turned into an entity, we shall nevertheless fail to achieve a just distribution of wealth because there is no rule by which we can determine the relative values of all different trades; that is, how much should an electrician earn compared to a farmer, doctor, actor, and teacher?[63]

Finally, Hayek believes that our vain attempt to establish a just pattern of financial rewards is bound to drive us closer to totalitarianism. Social justice is intervention in the market to achieve certain incomes for certain people. Thus, it will cause the failure of wages and prices to bring about a coordination of individual activities and this then will have to be done by central direction. Also, once government embarks on controlling wages for the benefit of some, it cannot, in justice, refuse to do it for all.

Though social justice has meaning only within a comprehensive organization, there is a particular conception of social justice that Hayek believes has been adopted by advocates of a market economy. This conception of social justice is based on moral merit and according to it people should be materially rewarded in correspondence with the amount of effort they expend. There are some advocates of a free market who defend the market precisely on the grounds that the market does accomplish this: that is, the market does reward the studious, hard working, and deserving.

Though there may be some correspondence between merit and reward, the remunerations of the market do not depend on an individual's merit but on the value of his services to other individuals. Hayek argues that a person's income can be influenced not only by effort or skill but by innate ability, luck, and accident. Though what a person accomplishes as a result of innate ability bears no relationship to moral merit, it nevertheless has value. If there are, say, two singers who each earn $100.00 a performance, their salaries do not reflect that one of them might have been born with his talent while the other had to struggle to train his voice. The market only considers the value of one's activities for others; it does not take into account individual merit in the sense of "effort of will or self-denial."[64] In fact, the entire idea that wages and prices are a reward for a past activity is erroneous. The purpose of prices is to guide individual economic activity in the present and future.[65] To achieve a distribution of income based on merit, someone will have to judge individual efforts and the function of prices will have to be perverted. This will destroy the self-generating order of the market.

Among free market defenders, Irving Kristol has raised an objection to Hayek's analysis. According to Kristol, Hayek's position is subversive of the social order. Historically, says Kristol, capitalism has been defended on the grounds that it is a just social order, that is, there is an intimate connection between moral merit and remunerations. By separating remunerations from moral merit, Hayek is destroying the legitimacy of capitalism. Individuals will not "accept a society in which power, privilege, and property are not distributed according to some morally meaningful criteria."[66]

Hayek responds to Kristol's criticisms in two ways. First, he simply denies the accuracy of Kristol's interpretation of history. With the exception of some early American authors, remunerations have not always been connected with moral merit. According to John Locke, and to the late schoolmen, especially L. Molina, it is the way that competition is conducted, and not its results, that can be described as just or unjust.[67] Second, Hayek argues that connecting the results of the market with moral merit will not necessarily make the results of the market more palatable. It may merely serve to give the businessman "an air of self-righteousness" which will hardly "make him more popular."[68]

Besides distribution according to merit, much of the concern for social justice involves considerations of equality and inequality. A great many people apparently believe that an inequality of material possessions, among different people, is simply unjust. There is no reason why some people should have more than others, and the government should act so as to either establish equality or at least lower the degree of inequality. Though he does not seem to be opposed to equality intrinsically, for example, if it should come about spontaneously, Hayek does not believe that the government should necessarily promote material equality. He attributes the belief that inequalities are unjust to the view that there is somebody who distributes goods and that it is this person's decision that has given one person more than another. If there is somebody who distributes all rewards for all tasks, it is possible to ask for justice from this person, and if this is the case perhaps equality would be a suitable starting place.[69] However, the market is not a thinking and acting being and attempts to use the coer-

cive powers of government to achieve a smaller difference between rich and poor are bound to have some unappealing economic and political consequences.

Though material inequality may appear to be unjust, and
perhaps even the cause of poverty, it is actually conducive to
material progress and the alleviation of poverty. As new goods
are developed, they are generally very expensive and initially
they can be supplied only to a few people. With the passage of
time, we learn how to make the goods more cheaply, and we
are then able to supply these goods more broadly among the
population. If we level inequalities, progress will come to a stop.
Even in a planned economy, if we want to maintain progress,
there will have to be inequality. Anent inequality, the only
difference between a market economy and a planned economy
would be that in the former inequalities would be determined
by the market process while in a planned economy inequalities would be determined politically. Though at any point in
time we can temporarily alleviate poverty by deliberately redistributing income, in the long run this will slow material
progress and thus harm everyone, rich and poor. Since the
population of the world is large and apparently increasing, if
we take measures that slow material progress, we shall not be
able to permanently alleviate poverty among the current population, much less support any increase in population.[70]

The attempt to level inequalities will also have serious political consequences. Hayek writes that there are two distinct
and mutually exclusive types of equality: equality before the
law and material equality. According to liberal tradition,
equality before the law helps to secure individual liberty by
preventing the discriminatory treatment of individuals by
government. The government cannot possibly achieve material equality among individuals that differ in abilities, interests, opportunities, and backgrounds by treating each of them
equally but only by treating each of them differently. Therefore, any governmental attempt to achieve material equality
will abrogate equality before the law, or, as Hayek sometimes
says, the Rule of Law. All attempts at any type of distributive
justice must lead to the gradual destruction of a device that
has been defended for centuries by liberal thinkers as a nec-

essary condition for individual freedom and the suppression of arbitrary power.[71]

Moreover, like any government intervention in the market to control wages and prices, the attempt to achieve material equality will destroy the function of prices and thus the market order. To achieve material equality, the market will have to be replaced by a command economy.

Though the argument against material equality is widely recognized among supporters of the market system, there is a particular type of equality that is favored by some votaries of the market system that is just as likely to lead to totalitarianism. This is equality of opportunity. The demand for equality of opportunity means that in starting life equality should be the rule and that a person's endeavors and accomplishments will then determine a person's station in life.

Hayek argues that a person's initial chances in life are determined by many physical and social circumstances and to ensure that everyone's initial chances are equal the government would have to control each of these circumstances. If the government is unable to provide everyone with an opportunity that is available to someone else, it will have to prevent people from taking advantage of their special opportunities. This will not only give the government an arbitrary power over the lives of individuals but it will vitiate the rationale of the market order which encourages people to make use of opportunities that may not be available to others.[72]

The demand for equality of opportunity calls for the most minute control of all actions and circumstances. If carried far enough, it could lead to the destruction of family life. Inequalities of opportunities could arise from the decisions of past generations. Even a decision on where to live may affect a person's initial chances, and, in part, parents may make such a decision on the basis of the perceived effect this will have on their offspring. If equality of opportunity is sought, either the government will have to make such a decision or it will have to control all circumstances that might cause one area to give greater chances of prosperity than others.[73]

The demand for equality of opportunity seems to be especially concerned with education and inheritance. Though Hayek argues that the quest for equality of opportunity could have undesirable effects, he is not opposed to the public financing of education in order to provide an education to the young that their guardians might not be able to afford. However, he does not believe that this is equality of opportunity. It appears that he would not oppose establishing a certain level or quality of education that would be provided for each child, but he would probably object if those who could provide themselves with a more extensive education were prohibited from doing so.[74]

Though inheriting money from one's family is a benefit that may disturb equality of opportunity, Hayek is not in favor of prohibiting the passing of estates from one generation to the next simply because this may produce inequality. Hayek argues that there are many different kinds of benefits that a family can supply to its offspring, such as the "transmission of morals, tastes, and knowledge," and there is no more reason to prevent the transfer of material goods that may cause inequalities than there is to prevent the transfer of non-material goods that may cause inequalities.[75]

The subject of inheritance, however, does raise an interesting issue. How successful is Hayek in articulating the principle by which income is actually distributed in a free market? According to Robert Nozick, Hayek argues against all types of patterned distributions, and particularly against the popular one of distribution according to merit. Yet, all Hayek does is to replace a distribution patterned upon merit with a "distribution in accordance with the perceived benefits to others, leaving room for the complaint that a free society does not realize exactly this pattern." Moreover, says Nozick, the principle that Hayek applies to explain the distribution of income, that is, value to others, does not apply to all types of income in a free society, "namely, inheritance, gifts for arbitrary reasons, charity, and so on."[76] Nozick is right. The principle that Hayek uses to explain the distribution of income does not apply to all types of income.

The principle guiding Hayek's complaints against attempts to redistribute income according to some pattern, for example, merit or equality, is that these endeavors will distort the market mechanism and eventually will lead to a complete break-

down of the market order. As we have noted, Hayek is not opposed to all welfare state activity but only to the types of
activity that distort the market mechanism. But a problem
arises here. Just as some types of welfare state activities are
outside the market, so are some types of income. If the state
taxes gifts and estates to achieve greater material equality,
what effect will this have on relative prices? The income one
receives from inheritance and gifts is outside the market
mechanism. Thus, Hayek's principle does not apply to this sort
of income. If it is Hayek's purpose to find a principle that explains the factual distribution of income in a society based on
voluntary exchange, he does not succeed. If it is Hayek's intention to discover a principle that prevents government from
redistributing income, his attempt is, at best, only a partial
success. It is not that Hayek does not argue against using inheritance taxes to prevent inequality. He does. And it is not
that some of his arguments are not powerful. They are. But
rather, it is simply that his principle does not apply to income
that is determined outside the market.[77]

Equality in the distribution of material goods, and distribution according to merit, are both general types of social justice. In *The Mirage of Social Justice,* Hayek discusses two
particular arguments that are advanced in the name of social
justice. We shall consider the most important argument of the
two.

Hayek is concerned with the idea that certain groups should
be allowed to protect the positions they achieve in the market
by determining their remunerations politically instead of economically. What Hayek means is that a doctor, a lawyer, a
farmer, or whatever will become accustomed to making X dollars an hour. If circumstances change and they make less than
X dollars an hour, they will regard this as unjust. Since they
are working as diligently as they previously did, they believe
that it is only just that they continue to earn the same amount
of money. Powerful groups in such a position will attempt to
have the political authorities fix their salaries at their accustomed rate, or will join together to fix their own remunerations. This they call social justice.

This, Hayek argues, is not justice, and it will lead to the destruction of the market. Since changes in wages and prices indicate that circumstances have changed, the fixing of particular wages will distort the informational function of prices and encourage activities that should be discouraged. It is only where wages are allowed to fall that one will be able to discover that he should redirect his efforts.[78]

The fixing of benefits for some cannot be extended to all and it is therefore a privilege. Those that attempt to fix their wages have attained their position only because of circumstances and the rules of the market. If those who prospered as a result of circumstances and the rules of the market attempt to prevent others from prospering from the same factors, this is not social justice. This is "eminently unjust."[79]

Social justice, for Hayek, is coming more and more to mean protecting the relative and absolute incomes of particular groups, as, for example, parity for the farmer. Since this treatment cannot be extended to all, it is usually reserved for politically powerful groups that can manipulate the legislative process. As we shall see in chapter five, Hayek regards this as such a serious problem that he attempts to revise democratic institutions so that groups will not be able to use the legislative process to destroy the market.

THE MARKET ORDER

The market, like society, is an order and a very complicated order. This order is based upon many separate individuals taking account of many particular facts which by their very nature cannot all be known to any one source. In essence, all attempts to control the market are based on intellectual error. Implicitly, it is assumed that all order is man-made, or at least that a man-made order is superior to all others, and that there is thus a creator and a purpose to all order.

Hayek suggests that it is a misuse of some of our terms that leads us to a misunderstanding of the market order. Though the word economy is used to describe the free market, it is a misnomer. The term economy refers to an order which uses means for specific ends. The free market is not an economy but more accurately a relationship among many economies. In reference to the free market, Hayek suggests that we abandon the term economy and instead substitute a term that describes the market order as a relationship between many economies. The term he suggests is "catallaxy."[80]

A catallaxy is end-independent, an economy is not. Hayek insists that we cannot rank ends in a large and open society without threatening freedom, peace, and progress. In an economy, all collaboration must take place on the basis of agreement on ends, and if, as is likely when we are dealing with many individuals, agreement is absent, force will be exerted to determine what should be done and who should do it. In a catallaxy, we often collaborate, freely and peaceably, with others even when we do not agree with their ends and even when we do not know of their ends.

Presumably, for Hayek, both an economy and a catallaxy have the same function. Each solves, or attempts to solve, the problem of providing for needs. In an economy, the attempt is made by deciding on what needs to meet and directing individuals to meet these needs. The catallaxy is far more complicated and can provide for far more needs.

Hayek suggests viewing the catallaxy as a wealth-producing game. Like any game, it is conducted according to rules and concluded by a combination of skill and luck. By participating in this game, a player can satisfy needs of which he is ignorant because prices indicate where his services are most useful.[81]

The game of catallaxy brings about the most efficient use of resources and the greatest amount of wealth possible. It does this in two ways. First, it gives the information and the incentives necessary to take advantage of special circumstances. Second, and perhaps even more importantly, the game of catallaxy encourages the use of the smallest amount of resources possible. Prices encourage each individual to economize on the use of resources in production. This means that resources will be available for more production than would otherwise be the case.[82]

The results of the game of catallaxy will be different for different people. A combination of luck and skill will determine the outcome. Even the initial chances of different individuals will be different. None of this, however, means that the resulting distribution of wealth is unjust. The game of catallaxy tends to produce as much total wealth as is possible and it improves everyone's chances. As long as no one distributes wealth, as long as the rules of the game apply equally to all, the resulting distribution is not unjust. Though government policy cannot aim at achieving any specific results for any particular individuals, the government can change certain rules so that any randomly chosen person will have a greater chance of achieving his aims.[83]

In his discussion of the meaning of society, Hayek says that there are two different types of society, a tribal society and a great society.[84] Unlike a great society, a tribal society is a small homogeneous grouping of individuals that existed in the distant past. In the small group that Hayek calls tribal society, there is general agreement on ends and the society is so small that it can be effectively organized on the lines of command and obedience. But the opposite is the case with a great society. In a great society, needs are various and unperceived. In contrast to a tribal society, people are led to serve others by promoting their own good.[85] The proponents of socialism, interventionism, and social justice, and those who uncomprehendingly scoff at Adam Smith's description of the invisible hand do not realize that there is an order in the world other than that which man creates.[86] And they do not realize that their ideals are the ideals of a past age when life was less complicated. In a society where the number of people is large and interdependence among the people is great, only an abstract order will allow for the fulfillment of needs. It is not the proponents of a free market who view modern life simplistically and nostalgically but rather those who believe a great society can be governed in the manner of a tribal society.

SUMMARY AND CONCLUSION

We shall close this chapter with a discussion of Professor Christian Bay's criticisms of Hayek's economic doctrine. A brief analysis of Bay's criticisms will allow us to consider briefly some aspects of Hayek's economic thought that have not been central to our presentation, and it will also allow us to emphasize some aspects of Hayek's thought that are central to our discussion.

Professor Bay has a long list of criticisms. Hayek, says Bay, is a laissez-faire theorist, and though this sort of theory may have had some validity a century or two ago, it is today inapplicable because, as Hayek fails to realize, a free market does not exist, and monopolies and oligopolies now rule the economy.[87] Unlike these charges, most of Bay's criticisms have a moral rather than a technical foundation. Hayek is "a special pleader," his "enemies are the champions of the poor and his aim is to perpetuate for others the blessings of the existing system."[88] Hayek wants a type of freedom in which the wealthy are at liberty to take advantage of the poor. Indeed, his terms "evoke the spirit of liberty not of a Socrates but of a Callicles or a Thrysymachus [sic]."[89] So unconcerned with the welfare of the poor is Hayek, that, says Bay, he "reminds me of Rousseau's example of the philosopher who could go back to sleep after a murder had been committed under his window."[90] After citing a passage in which Hayek argues that both peace and the economic development of poor nations depend in part on the further economic development of wealthier nations, Professor Bay reaches this startling illation: "Let's use our elbows, then, and our napalm when necessary, and keep 'progressing' ahead of the rest; this is the nature of a competitive world order, corresponding to the nature of competition in the free society of Manchester liberals."[91]

Though Bay is critical of Hayek, there are times when he mingles his criticism with praise. For example, though Hayek is dedicated to allowing the wealthy to benefit at the expense of the poor, Bay assures us that Hayek "is not in favor of poverty." In another passage, Bay quite clearly informs his readers that Hayek is not a fascist.[92]

We shall now discuss some of Bay's charges. First, is Hayek an exponent of laissez-faire theory? Hayek characterizes his own position as anti-socialist, which, he says, means that he rejects market intervention. This, he says, is not laissez-faire. By extrapolating from his argument, it seems that he reserves the term laissez-faire for theories that limit the tasks of the state, especially those that would limit it to the prevention of violence (foreign and domestic), what some might be inclined to call the minimal state. This, Hayek seems to think, is laissez-faire, and this, he also believes, does not describe his position because he gives the state a number of tasks that go beyond merely preserving peace.[93] Thus, we can conclude that if laissez-faire is defined as opposition to market intervention, then Hayek is a laissez-faire theorist. If it is defined in terms of limiting state activities to narrow functions, then he is not a laissez-faire theorist. However this may be, we should note in passing that another free market economist, von Mises, seems to use the first definition of laissez-faire.[94]

Next, is Hayek oblivious to the imperfections of the market? Is he oblivious to problems created by monopolies, oligopolies, and, more generally, corporations? Is his theory based on the assumption of perfect competition? Hayek has been writing on the problems of market imperfections for approximately five decades. Though one may legitimately disagree with Hayek, any analysis of his economic thought that suggests that he is unaware of market imperfections, or that he does not take them into account, is highly misleading. Indeed, his entire career as an economist is marked by his concern that the market is being progressively destroyed.[95] Since we are mainly concerned with Hayek's principles, we shall merely summarize his position on market imperfections. Though we cannot go through all the fine points, I do think that we can at least show that Hayek has taken account of market imperfections.

Hayek believes that the free market is often condemned because the market of the real world does not correspond to the theory of perfect competition. The theory of perfect competition, however, is merely a construction by economists to explain how the market works. This type of analysis can be very misleading. Above all, competition is a discovery procedure (he compares competition in the market with competition in sports and examinations, where we have competition because we do not know the results before hand), it is a procedure which discovers unknowns (e.g., the most efficient size of a firm, and the lowest cost of production for a commodity). Unlike competition in the market, the theory of perfect competition is a static analysis in which the unknowns are assumed to be known. Competition in the market, however, is a dynamic process, and the theory of perfect competition "leaves no room whatever for the activity called competition, which is presumed to have already done its task."[96] As a result of competition, monopolies will sometimes arise. But where monopoly is the result of superior efficiency, it is not necessarily harmful because the commodity that is being produced is being produced as cheaply as anyone else can produce it and it is being sold at a price which is below that at which any competitor can sell it. Thus, what is important is that there is free entry and no artificial barriers to competition.[97]

Though Hayek feels that monopolies which arise because of superior efficiency are not necessarily harmful, he also says that not all monopolies arise in this manner and that many firms that have market power have it as a result of privileges granted by government. These monopolies we can and should do something about. Hayek believes that government grants privileges to labor unions that distort the market mechanism and he therefore urges reforms in our labor laws.[98] Tariffs, progressive taxation, corporate taxation, government aid to large firms, our current laws on patents and copyrights, all encourage market concentration and he therefore also urges reforms in these areas.[99] In some fields, like postal service and transport, governments actually create monopoly.[100] Hayek believes that the rules which govern economic organization and behavior can be either good or bad, and he believes that we can improve the economic order by changing and improving our law. For example, in regard to corporations, he suggests that each individual stockholder should be allowed to decide what part of his profits will be reinvested in the corporation. He also suggests that one corporation should never have voting rights in another corporation.[101] Of course, one may say that Hayek's account of market imperfections is unimpressive. But surely, he does take account of such imperfections.

Bay's charge that Hayek has a class bias and that his intention is to perpetuate the social positions of the rich and the poor shows a complete lack of understanding of Hayek's political philosophy. First, as we have pointed out, Hayek believes it is one of the greatest threats to freedom that the government actually prevents the decline of politically powerful groups from the positions of wealth that they have attained. But even if Hayek had not made that particular argument, one could deduce from his central argument that he is not interested in perpetuating anyone's position. In fact, his entire argument leads to exactly the opposite conclusion. The market order is an abstract order in which, if the order is to be maintained, the positions of the different individuals must change. Positions change in response to prices. Prices are of preeminent importance in understanding Hayek's political philosophy. It is because of a functioning price system that resources will be allocated efficiently. It is also because of a functioning price system that central direction is unnecessary and individuals are free to pursue their own goals. Prices must be allowed to function in order to achieve prosperity and freedom. Yet if prices are allowed to function, the position of different individuals will change. Indeed, individual positions cannot be guaranteed in a free market. Since prices play such a paramount role in Hayek's political philosophy, it might be thought that Professor Bay would devote the better part of his article to an analysis of the function of prices. He does not. He devotes only two paragraphs to prices, and these two paragraphs do not convey the sense that he understands the importance that Hayek attaches to prices.[102] And without understanding the importance of prices in Hayek's political philosophy, one cannot understand Hayek's argument.

Concerning Hayek's lack of concern for the impoverished, Hayek argues that a functioning market will alleviate poverty as much as possible. Bay refers to this argument as a "thin humanistic veneer."[103] However, we should note that Hayek shares his opinion with some other students of economics. According to Schumpeter, "the capitalist achievement does not typically consist in providing more silk stockings for queens but in bringing them within the reach of factory girls in return for steadily decreasing amounts of effort."[104] Also, Hayek says that where people are unable to procure a living within the market the government can provide for them outside the market in the form of a minimum level of income. Hayek is not opposed to government aid to the poor. He is opposed to government intervention in the market.[105]

Though Professor Bay's criticisms are of aid in putting Hayek's philosophy in perspective in regard to such things as market imperfections, social mobility, and the alleviation of poverty in a free society, they are in their own right a failure. He surely tells us where he believes Hayek is in error, but he rarely adduces evidence in support of his positions. All too often he resorts to name calling, for instance, associating Hayek with Callicles and Thrasymachus. However, Bay's use of these names reminds me of a passage in the *Gorgias* where Socrates and Polus are engaged in an argument. After Socrates advances an argument, Polus begins to laugh. Socrates says, "What's this, Polus? Laughing? Is this a new type of proof, laughing at what your opponent says instead of giving reasons?"[106] Perhaps Polus and Bay are both inventors of new types of proof.

The free market is an abstract order. In a great society, individual freedom and economic efficiency depend on this abstract order. This abstract order depends on prices. Any intervention in the market impairs the function of prices and thus causes economic inefficiency. Any act of intervention is an act of arbitrary coercion and is objectionable merely on this account. But there is more to it than this. If every act of intervention is not ruled out in principle, we are setting the stage for a series of acts of intervention that in their totality will fully destroy freedom. As prices fail to function as a direct result of intervention, we shall reach a stage when prices no longer direct resources. The proponents of intervention may well be among the first to come to the conclusion that the market does not function. They will probably attribute the failure of the market to some law of historical inevitability rather than to their own actions.

Such at any rate is Hayek's opinion. Perhaps he is in error. But to ascertain this, someone will have to refute his argument, and this will probably have to be done in the conventional manner of providing a counter argument. The more novel proofs of Polus and Bay may not be conclusive.

NOTES

1. For Hayek's view of society, see Hayek, 1973c, pp. 8–54; Hayek, 1964a; Hayek, 1952a; Hayek, 1967b, pp. 66–81, 96–105.

2. Hayek, 1973c, p. 18.

3. Though he says that rules are necessary for a spontaneous order, Hayek also argues that not all rules will produce an order. See Hayek, 1973c, p. 44. Also Hayek, 1967b, p. 67.

4. Hayek, 1973c, pp. 20–21. Also Hayek, 1967b, pp. 96–97.

5. Hayek, 1964a, p. 10. Also Hayek, 1973c, pp. 45, 47–48.

6. In Hayek, 1973c, p. 148 n. 14, Hayek comments on the inability of computers to account for all the facts on which the social order is based.

7. Hayek, 1973c, pp. 48–51.

8. Hayek, 1979, p. xii.

9. Hayek, 1944, pp. 32, 56. Hayek, 1948, p. 129. Hayek, 1960a, pp. 253–254. Hayek's definition of socialism does not appear to differ much from that offered by some socialists. "A state so designated is here understood as being one in which the control of the whole apparatus of production and the guidance of all productive operations is to be in the hands of the state itself." Taylor, 1970, p. 43.

10. Hayek, 1948, pp. 92–106, 121, 123, 131.

11. Hayek, 1948, p. 94. Hayek, 1978c, pp. 179–190.

12. Hayek argues that we have economic problems only as a result of change. Hayek, 1948, pp. 81–83, 157. On the same point, see von Mises, 1951, pp. 139, 196–204.

13. Hayek, 1948, p. 80.

14. Hayek, 1948, pp. 54, 77, 91. Also Hayek, 1978c, p. 236.

15. Hayek, 1948, p. 87.

16. Hayek, 1948, pp. 85–87.

17. Lange, 1970, esp. pp. 73, 83, 89.

18. Hayek, 1948, pp. 181–208. Also see pp. 119–180 of the same work.

19. Hayek, 1948, p. 176.

20. See Hayek, 1978c, p. 20. However, compare this with statements in Hayek, 1941a, p. 81, and Hayek, 1948, p. 176.

21. Hayek, 1948, pp. 162–172, 194–195.

22. Hayek, 1948, pp. 177, 186. Also Hayek, 1978c, p. 304.

23. Hayek, 1978c, p. 305. Also see pp. 232, 237, of the same work.

24. Schumpeter, 1950, part 3.

25. von Mises, 1935, ch 3.

26. Schumpeter, 1950, p. 175.

27. Hayek, 1948, p. 90. Also see von Mises, 1949, p. 354.

28. Wallich, 1960, p. 21.

29. This seems to be suggested by Wooton, 1945, pp. 16, 110–115.

30. Hayek, 1944, p. 206.

31. Hayek, 1944, pp. 33–34, 56.

32. Hayek, 1944, pp. xvii, xxi, 3, 5, 137. Also Hayek, 1978c, p. 296.

33. Hayek, 1944, pp. 34–35. Hayek, 1978c, p. 233.

34. Hayek, 1944, p. 57.

35. Hayek, 1944, p. 222.

36. Hayek, 1944, pp. 54, 153, 156, 222. One may wonder about the effect that Hayek believes democracy will have on socialism. Though ch. 5 will consider his views on government, there is one point that can be mentioned here. Hayek believes that democracy will be virtually impossible in a socialist state. He advances two arguments to support this thesis. First, economic management will become so difficult that the assembly will have to delegate an extraordinary amount of power to the bureaucracy. Second, since planning will have to be in detail, a majority will rarely exist on any issue. Rather than majority rule, it will be rule by the largest minority. Hayek believes that these minorities will be very small. He also believes that socialism will eventually lead to dictatorship. See Hayek, 1944, pp. 56–71. Also see Arnold Brecht's rather interesting discussion of what he refers to as the "Lenin-Hayek theory." Brecht, 1959, pp. 449–453.

37. Hayek, 1944, pp. 42, 199.

38. Hayek, 1955b, p. 48; Hayek, 1944, pp. 94–96.

39. Hayek, 1944, pp. 101, 106–108.

40. Hayek, 1944, p. 91; Hayek, 1978c, p. 149.

41. Hayek, 1944, pp. 85–86.

42. Hayek, 1944, p. 93.

43. Friedman, 1962, pp. 16–18. Also, see what Hayek means by "the man of independent means" in Hayek, 1960a, p. 125.

44. Hayek, 1948, p. 206.

45. Heilbroner, 1967, p. 254.

46. Brecht, 1959, p. 452.

47. Nozick, 1974, pp. 160–164.

48. Milton Friedman makes an observation that is similar to Nozick's. Friedman argues that the market may be universal. He says that even in the Soviet Union all goods and services are not produced by the state. For example, an electrician that needs plumbing help will make arrangements with a plumber outside the state apparatus by promising his services to the plumber in exchange. One can conclude from Friedman's observation that either the government of the

Soviet Union is not powerful enough to prevent private economic transactions or that it is unwilling to use this power. Friedman's observation was made on a television interview for which I unfortunately do not have a reference. However, there is a discussion of this topic in "Living Conveniently on the Left", in *Time*, June 23, 1980, p. 50.

49. For Tawney's criticisms of Hayek and for his own analysis of the subject under consideration see Tawney, 1953, pp. 91–99.

50. Hayek, 1960a, p. 254.

51. Hayek, 1960a, p. 286.

52. Hayek, 1960a, p. 343.

53. Hayek, 1973c, p. 57.

54. Hayek, 1973c, p. 58.

55. Hayek, 1973c, p. 61.

56. Hayek, 1979, pp. 150–151.

57. Hayek, 1960a, p. 256.

58. Hayek, 1976e, pp. 64–65. Also Hayek, 1978c, pp. 57–68.

59. Hayek, 1976e, pp. 31–32.

60. Hayek, 1976e, p. 93.

61. Hayek, 1976e, pp. 103–106.

62. Hayek, 1976e, p. 104.

63. Hayek, 1976e, pp. 64–65, 77–78; Hayek, 1978c, p. 58.

64. Hayek, 1960a, p. 94.

65. Hayek, 1976e, pp. 71–72.

66. Kristol, 1972, p. 97.

67. Hayek, 1976e, pp. 73–74, 178–179; Hayek, 1973c, pp. 21, 150 n. 22; Hayek, 1978c, pp. 28, 255.

68. Hayek, 1976e, p. 74.

69. Hayek, 1976e, pp. 80–81.

70. Hayek, 1960a, pp. 42–49. Also Hayek, 1978c, p. 65.

71. Hayek, 1944, p. 79; Hayek, 1960a, p. 87.

72. Hayek, 1976e, pp. 10, 82, 84–85.

73. Hayek, 1976e, pp. 9–10, 87–88.

74. Hayek, 1976e, p. 84. Also see Hayek, 1960a, pp. 376–394.

75. Hayek, 1960a, p. 90.

76. Nozick, 1974, p. 158.

77. However, we should note that Hayek does seem to be aware that his principle does not apply to inheritance. In fact, it appears that at one time Hayek supported the use of estate taxes to achieve greater equality. See Hayek, 1948, p. 118. Also see Hayek, 1960a, p. 91.

78. Hayek, 1976e, pp. 93–94.

79. Hayek, 1976e, p. 95.

80. Hayek, 1976e, pp. 108–109. Others, as Hayek notes, also use the term catallactics to describe the market order, e.g., von Mises, 1949, p. 233.

81. Hayek, 1976e, pp. 115–116. On p. 125 of the same work, Hayek compares the function of prices to negative feedback in cybernetics. Also see Hayek, 1978c, p. 63.

82. Hayek, 1976e, pp. 117–118.

83. Hayek, 1976e, p. 114.

84. Hayek, 1973c, p. 14. Also see Hayek, 1977, pp. 6–7.

85. By pursuing one's own good, Hayek does not mean selfishness or egoism. See Hayek, 1976e, p. 145. Also Hayek, 1978c, pp. 268–269.

86. Hayek, 1978c, p. 63.

87. Bay, 1971, pp. 110, 118–119.

88. Bay, 1971, pp. 110, 113, 93.

89. Bay, 1971, p. 113. Also see pp. 94, 112.

90. Bay, 1971, p. 110.

91. Bay, 1971, p. 116.

92. Bay, 1971, pp. 113, 121.

93. Hayek, 1978c, p. 306. Also see Hayek, 1944, pp. 17–19, 36; Hayek, 1960a, pp. 60, 231; Hayek, 1979, p. 41; Hayek, 1948, p. 134.

94. von Mises, 1949, pp. 725–727.

95. Hayek, 1948, p. 136.

96. Hayek, 1978c, p. 182. In the same work, see pp. 179–181, 184–185. Also see Hayek, 1948, pp. 92, 94–97, 102, 106; Hayek, 1955b, p. 59; Hayek, 1967b, pp. 176, 288; Hayek, 1979, pp. 65, 67, 69–70, 77–78.

97. Hayek, 1944, p. 48; Hayek, 1948, pp. 100, 104–105; Hayek, 1960a, p. 65; Hayek, 1967b, p. 288; Hayek, 1978c, p. 185; Hayek, 1979, pp. 67, 73–74, 80, 83.

98. Hayek, 1960a, p. 267–284. Also Hayek, 1980. For a critical discussion of Hayek's proposed labor reforms, see Barry, 1979, pp. 74–75.

99. Hayek, 1948, pp. 113, 114; Hayek, 1955b, p. 58; Hayek, 1960a, pp. 317, 320; Hayek, 1967b, pp. 176, 286; Hayek, 1978c, p. 146; Hayek, 1979, pp. 82–83, 88.

100. Hayek, 1979, pp. 56–59, 88.

101. Hayek, 1967b, pp. 308–309.

102. Bay, 1971, pp. 117, 119.

103. Bay, 1971, p. 116.

104. Schumpeter, 1950, p. 67.

105. Hayek, 1976e, p. 87.

106. Plato, 1960, p. 61.

IV.

Freedom and the Law

According to Hayek, there are two different traditions in liberal political thought concerning law. Some theorists, like Jeremy Bentham, emphasize that laws are an abridgment of freedom, other theorists, Immanuel Kant, for example, emphasize that laws are a necessary and essential condition of freedom. Though political theorists differ on the relationship between law and liberty, this is so, believes Hayek, only because they differ on the meaning of the term law.[1] Hayek argues that the word law has a definite meaning, and only if it is properly understood can it be said that law protects individual freedom. In this chapter, we shall present Hayek's legal philosophy, and since Hayek attaches such a great significance to the meaning of the word law, we shall primarily be interested in the way that Hayek uses the term and why he believes that law in this sense is conducive to a condition of individual liberty. Since Hayek's most recent analysis of law seems to differ in certain respects from his earlier analysis of law (some of these differences will be noted toward the end of this chapter), we shall focus on his most recent exposition of law in *Law, Legislation and Liberty*.

THE ORIGIN OF LAW

In the beginning of the previous chapter, it was shown that Hayek believes that there are two types of order and that each type of order is formed by a corresponding system of rules. The first type of order he refers to as a cosmos and the other as a taxis. Unlike a taxis, which is a created order, a cosmos is a self-generating order that is formed by a multitude of people interacting with each other according to abstract rules which arise in an evolutionary manner.

Since the advent of modern legislation, which Hayek dates as beginning in the thirteenth century, man has regarded law as the deliberate creation of government. However, throughout most prior history, the laws of human conduct, like those of nature, were thought to be independent of human volition. Initially, government did not create law but was legitimized by articulating, interpreting, and enforcing a pre-existing system of justice. Since law is no longer seen as an evolutionary growth, and thus as existing independently of human will, some people do not see law as limiting political power.[2]

Though, in the sense of changing or creating rules of conduct, government has not always had the power to legislate, it has always had the power to legislate in the sense of creating rules of organization or determining public policy. As the government came to have the power of altering two entirely different types of laws, the distinction between them became obliterated and just as government has always had complete power over the rules of organization, it came to be thought that government also has complete power over the rules of human conduct.[3]

As the term law came to be applied to both rules of conduct and the power of directing government, these two activities became indistinguishable. The only place this did not occur was in England. It was there that the ideal of liberty under the law developed. What prevented the confusion of the two types of law in England was the common law. Though Montesquieu attributed the liberty of the English as due to a separation of powers between parliament and king, the existence of liberty was due to the common law which was developed by the courts independently of either parliament or king, both of whom were mainly concerned with organizing and directing government.[4]

It is in the common law (which Hayek also refers to as nomos, evolutionary law, private law, civil law, and judge-made law) that Hayek believes we shall find protection from unlimited political power. He believes that the common law, as a necessary result of its evolutionary development, possesses special attributes and that legislation must take the common law as its model if liberty is not to be destroyed.

PRIVATE LAW

In his discussion of law, Hayek divides law into two broad types, public law (which he also calls thesis) and private law. He further divides private law into criminal law and civil law. It is the private law, and particularly the civil law, that is responsible for the creation of an order of peace and liberty.[5] The distinction that Hayek draws between private law and public law is virtually identical to the distinction that he draws between the rules of conduct that form a cosmos and the rules of organization that form a taxis. The importance of private law is that it is conducive to the formation of an order that he designates a catallaxy. Since it has been shown in the previous chapter why a catallaxy is conducive to freedom and prosperity, we shall not repeat that explanation here, but we shall accept Hayek's opinions on the market order as given and attempt to show the importance of private law in the formation and maintenance of this order.

For a self-generating order to form, private property and rules defining the conditions for the acquisition and transference of property are necessary. Private property allows individuals to use means to promote their own ends, and the law serves as an instrument that enables us to determine who is entitled to use particular means. By determining the boundaries of property, the law prohibits interference in the use of means and empowers each of us to know what resources we are free to use in the pursuit of our goals. Thus, in a society in which there is no comprehensive agreement on ends, the law provides for peace and liberty by serving a multiplicity of ends. Since the law is merely a set of prohibitions concerning means, the individual is free in the choice of his ends. A system of private law forms the foundation of an abstract order precisely because it makes it possible for a multitude of people to seek their own individual ends.[6]

The private law, says Hayek, develops by a process of evolution. Since law develops by such a process, it has certain attributes that are essential for the formation of a spontaneous order and thus for individual liberty.

Society and law come into existence simultaneously. A society does not give itself laws, rather, a society is a pattern of activities that is based on the observance of laws.[7] Any political authority that comes into existence finds a pre-existing pattern of activities, and thus rules that are conducive to this pattern of activities, already existing. Individuals come to form certain expectations concerning the actions of other individuals, that is, they expect other individuals to act in accordance with the rules. However, there will often be disputes about the law. There will be disagreements on the interpretation of the law, disagreements concerning what law should apply to a particular case, a dispute may start because a totally new set of circumstances arises to which there is no law, or some individuals may simply refuse to obey the law. Thus, the prime purpose of government, or more particularly a judge, will be "to correct disturbances of an order that has not been made by anyone and does not rest on the individuals having been told what they must do."[8] The judge will correct this disturbance by articulating the principles that apply to particular cases.

The judge has the function of settling conflicts that arise between individuals. A litigant comes before a judge with the complaint that he has suffered harm as the result of some other party not observing the law. The judge decides the particular case by finding a rule that should have guided expectations in a particular case. In order to prevent future conflict in similar cases, when a judge decides a particular case he will have to state the general principle that leads him to his conclusion. It is only in this way that the judge can ensure that future conflicts of a similar nature will be avoided and that an order of actions will continue.[9]

Since the law arises by a process of evolution, that is, through

continuously settling individual cases where there is a dis-
agreement over the law, this inevitably causes the law to assume particular attributes. The first attribute of law is that it
deals with what Mill might call other-regarding activity. Hayek
explains that since a judge settles disputes between individuals, legal rules can pertain only to other-regarding activity
and that they cannot pertain to actions which affect only the
voluntary actor or those who voluntarily cooperate with him.[10]

In Hayek's earlier works on law, he was interpreted as saying that general rules ipso facto create sufficient conditions for
individual liberty. Some critics have pointed out that even
general rules can be extremely and unnecessarily coercive, for
example, rules requiring religious conformity. His explanation
that a judge is concerned with only other-regarding activity is
intended, he says, to negate this criticism.[11] However, in several different ways, his new formula raises problems. For example, if the law is truly concerned with actions that only affect other individuals, it is not clear how we can justifiably
prohibit cruelty to animals. Also, there is a problem of consistency. On the one hand, he says that voluntary actions that
affect only the voluntary actors can never become the concern
of a judge. On the other hand, in a number of his works, he
says that in principle there is nothing to object to in safety or
factory legislation.[12] Yet, there seems to be a problem here.
Can the state legitimately require an employer to provide his
employee with, for example, a gas mask (if the employee is
working with dangerous gases or chemicals) even if both voluntarily agree that such a piece of equipment need not be provided and if such a decision affects no one but the voluntary
actors? Can the state require professional boxers to wear six-
teen-ounce gloves rather than eight-ounce gloves? Can it prohibit boxing altogether? Hayek is not clear on questions like
these. If we reason from his principle, we shall come to the
conclusion that safety and factory legislation is unjustifiable
if it is intended to prevent harm only to voluntary actors.
However, if we reason from his acceptance of safety legislation, we shall not arrive at the principle he enunciates.

The second attribute of evolved law is that it is abstract.[13]
It is necessarily abstract because it is a statement of a prin-

ciple that not only applies to the particular case at hand but applies also to all future cases of a similar nature.

The third attribute of evolved law is that it is negative. With rare exceptions, the law does not impose positive duties on anyone.[14] Since the purpose of law is to keep peace among individuals with different ends, evolved law is likely to be negative. Moreover, it is very difficult to impose positive obligations on particular people by using abstract rules.

The leader of an organization does not fulfill the same function as a judge, and for this reason Hayek believes that created law does not necessarily have the same attributes as evolved law. All organizations, including government, aim at concrete ends. Since an organization seeks to achieve a particular end, the rules that emanate from an organization take on attributes that are necessary for that entity to achieve its end, that is, the rules are concrete and not abstract. Particular ends can be achieved only by directing particular individuals to do particular things. A judge is not interested in any particular result even where a particular concrete result seems desirable. A judge is interested only in discovering if actions are in accord with established rules, and he cannot be concerned with the particular result that comes from his decision. For example, in deciding a particular case between a rich man and a poor man, or between a charitable man and a miser, the judge can be concerned only with the rules governing the case at hand, and he cannot simply decide for the needy or the meritorious. Though the judge may prefer one particular result to another, his decision must be in accordance with the rules if that system of rules, and the resulting abstract order of actions, is to be maintained. Since the leader of an organization, unlike a judge, is interested in concrete ends, it is unlikely that he will create abstract rules. The attributes that result from created law are unlikely to be the same as those of evolved law. And without the attributes that evolved law necessarily possesses, the law will not be conducive to the formation of a spontaneous order of actions.[15]

Since a judge has the aim of preventing conflict, he must decide individual cases by articulating a principle that will apply to an unknown number of future cases. Moreover, the rule that he articulates in any particular case must be consistent with other rules or only disorder will result. Since the rules form the basis for an order of actions, the rules must be consistent with each other. Therefore, the judge must decide an individual case by stating a rule that will apply to similar future cases, and yet that rule must be consistent with an interrelated series of rules.[16]

Sometimes it is even possible that a court will have to deal with a conflict for which there is no established law for the judge to apply. In a case of this nature, the judge must nevertheless make a decision. Though, in a sense, the judge will be making new law, he is still not free to promulgate any rule he wishes. The rule that the judge articulates will still have to satisfy certain criteria; it will have to establish a principle that will apply to an unknown number of potential cases, and it will have to be consistent with an ongoing order of actions which is based on a system of rules. Thus, a judge does not actually make law but rather discovers law.[17]

Hayek also argues that judicial decisions are more predictable under a system of common law than they are under a statutory system. No legal code is ever complete in the sense that all of its principles have been stated. In a system of statutory law, a judge renders a decision from a limited number of written rules. However, a judge is more likely to satisfy expectations where he is free to make decisions according to the spirit of the law rather than according to the letter of the law, that is, where his decisions are based on an entire system of law of which each and every rule has not been stated rather than on a limited number of written rules.[18]

Although Hayek feels that a system of common law is superior to a system of statutory law, he is not prepared to argue for the complete abandonment of legislation in the field of private law. He offers two reasons for the preservation of legislation in private law. First, since judge-made law arises gradually, legislation may be necessary to expedite adjustments in the law to changing conditions. Second, and most important, judicial decisions in a particular area can move in the wrong direction, and a judge cannot reverse a precedent without disappointing legitimate expectations. In regard to overturning precedents, legislation is superior to judicial decision.[19]

Though I do not mean to say that Hayek's justification of legislation is implausible, it is, however, questionable whether or not his justification of it is compatible with his explanation of evolutionary law. First, he thinks legislation is necessary so that we can quickly adapt to changing circumstances. Yet the rationale of an evolutionary system would seem to be that we adapt to new circumstances slowly and in a piecemeal manner by constantly adjusting new rules to an entire system of rules. Second, he prefers legislators rather than judges to overturn precedents because it will not upset expectations. However, he prefers common law to statutory law because in the latter a judge is often limited to making his decisions by the letter of the law, while in the former he bases his decisions on the spirit of the law. If a precedent is inconsistent with an entire system of rules, it seems that a judge would have little alternative but to overturn it. If he did not, he certainly would not be acting in the spirit of the law, and by perpetuating a rule that is not consistent with other rules he would also be undermining that order of actions of which it is the function of law to preserve.

SOVEREIGNTY

Though, to a degree, Hayek is willing to justify legislation in private law, his emphasis is on the superiority of judge-made law over legislation. Hayek points out that not all law is the product of a legislature because he believes that modern man has reached the erroneous conclusion that all law is the result of legislation, and from this belief deduces two dangerous corollaries which comprise the theory of sovereignty.

The first of these is the belief that there must be a supreme legislator whose power cannot be limited, because this would require a still higher legislator, and so on in an infinite regress. The other is that anything laid down by that supreme legislator is law and only that which expresses his will is law.[20]

If sovereignty means unlimited power, Hayek, like other twentieth-century theorists, rejects the concept.[21] One can reach the conclusion that a legislator has unlimited power only if one starts with the premise that all law is created. But Hayek, of course, does not start out with this premise. An allegiance to government is based on the belief that government will act according to, and enforce, pre-existing opinions of justice, and the power of law-making is thus both justified and limited by opinion, and opinion refers not only to the method in which a law is enacted but it mainly refers to the attributes of law. It may indeed be true that a supreme legislature exists, but this only means that there is no organized political power above it, it does not mean that it is omnipotent.[22]

In regard to political affairs, Hayek seems to take an intellectualist position. Quite often, Hayek quotes some well-known remarks by David Hume and John Maynard Keynes to the effect that political action is determined by opinion.[23] Also, he tells us that Confucius supposedly stated that when words lose their meaning, individuals lose their liberty.[24] What will eventually lead us down the road to serfdom is a misuse of words, false beliefs, and a misunderstanding of the social order, for instance, confusing a catallaxy with an economy, failing to distinguish between private and public law, confusing democracy with freedom, believing that all law is created, and misunderstanding the effects of early capitalism. All this, I understand Hayek to mean, will affect our opinions of permissible governmental action. Thus, a climate of opinion that is based on erroneous intellectual foundations can lead to a state of unlimited political power.[25]

PUBLIC LAW

Besides private law, or nomos, Hayek believes that there is a second distinctive type of law that is often confused with private law. Though society is formed by private law, government is necessary to secure obedience to law, and to provide goods and services that cannot be provided by the market. In order to set up courts, provide services, and, in general, to achieve any particular purposes, government cannot operate by abstract rules, though, it can obey such rules. The government will need rules of organization that arrange individuals into a hierarchy by indicating their tasks, and the resources they can use to accomplish their tasks.[26] These rules of organization Hayek calls public law or thesis.

In his discussion of public law, Hayek enumerates three types of such law and contrasts each of them with rules of just conduct. Though constitutional law is often represented as the highest type of law, it is nevertheless public law and not private law. While private law regulates conduct between individuals, constitutional law allocates authority within government and limits governmental power.[27]

Financial legislation is a second type of public law. Unlike private law which is not intended to achieve any particular result, financial legislation, the amount of money which government raises and spends, is intended to achieve specific objectives. When a legislature authorizes an expenditure it is not making a rule of just conduct but rather it is instructing the executive to achieve a particular goal. There is nothing inherently wrong with government attempting to achieve a particular goal provided that in doing so it acts like any other organization and does not infringe the rules of just conduct. Though government expenditures are determined by particular circumstances and do not necessarily raise questions of justice, the way taxes are apportioned among individuals does raise such questions and must be determined by general rules of just conduct.[28]

The final type of public law that Hayek distinguishes from rules of just conduct is administrative law. Though administrative law has several meanings, it most often means regulations determining how governmental agencies should use public resources. As such, it differs from private law, and Hayek, of course, does not have any objections to administrative law. However, Hayek says that occasionally the term administrative law is used to describe a power over private individuals and their property that is not limited to general rules and that in this sense administrative law means that government agencies are not under the rules of just conduct in their dealings with private citizens. Hayek takes exception to this use of administrative law and argues that government, except in certain extreme situations, cannot have any discretionary power over private individuals and must be "subject to the same jurisdiction of the ordinary courts as any private citizen."[29] In his exposition, Hayek does not give any examples of administrative law in this last sense. However, from other discussions on the inappropriate uses of law, it appears that he is referring to any attempt by government to control prices or quantities of commodities and services.[30]

Hayek has been criticized for saying that government should not have discretionary power. However, we should point out that he is speaking about a particular type of discretionary power and not about all discretionary power. Kenneth Davis tells us that the president in foreign affairs does have and must have discretionary power.[31] He cites President Kennedy's handling of the Cuban missile crisis as an example of the use, and the necessary use, of discretionary power. In deciding whether we should ignore the missile bases in Cuba, or attempt to remove them by invasion, bombing, blockade, or by trading missile bases in Turkey for the bases in Cuba, Hayek would not argue that Kennedy did not have discretionary power or that he should not have had discretionary power. For all practical purposes, what Hayek is saying is that government and individuals each have property and that in their use of their property for their own concrete goals they each must have discretionary power. However, except under extraordinary circumstances, the government does not have a discretionary power over the property of private citizens. The government may have discretion in using the navy for a blockade or in trading missile bases, but, from all we have said about Hayek's legal philosophy, I think that Hayek might regard it as quite another matter if the government ordered private ship owners to establish a blockade or if the government attempted to trade, say, General Motors Corporation to the Soviet Union in order to have missiles removed from Cuba. Hayek is not saying that government should not have discretionary power. He is merely attempting to remove the private citizen and his property from the scope of discretionary government power.

THE CONFUSION OF PRIVATE LAW AND PUBLIC LAW

As the preceding paragraphs show, Hayek believes there is a difference between various acts of government and he believes that this distinction is becoming increasingly obfuscated. Hayek divides acts of government into two types, nomos and thesis. Nomos is a rule of just conduct (which may, but need not, have been made by government) which limits the range of actions of individuals and organizations, including government. Thesis is a rule in the sense that it is an instruction by the legislature to somebody to perform a particular action. The reason for the lack of distinction between thesis and nomos is, in part, that both "emanate from the same authority."[32] Since legislatures make both thesis and nomos, thesis and nomos are lumped together as law. To keep the distinction, Hayek urges the creation of a two branch legislature, one a government assembly that gives directions to the executive and the other a legislative assembly that makes rules of conduct. However, we shall consider this suggestion only in the following chapter. Now, we shall outline Hayek's reasons for believing that a legislature that is predominantly concerned with thesis will destroy liberty.

If the distinction between thesis and nomos is not maintained, Hayek believes that thesis will increasingly destroy nomos and that a spontaneous order will be replaced by a totalitarian organization. If thesis is regarded as on a par with nomos, or if it is indistinguishable from nomos, every time the legislature decides a particular matter its decision will be regarded as law and if its decision is in conflict with a previously existing general rule its decision will override the general rule. Thus, general rules are in danger of being progressively replaced.[33]

One of the causes, believes Hayek, of the progressive replacement of nomos by thesis is the attempt by government to achieve certain social goals. All of our social goals, for example, certain attempts to alleviate poverty, do not necessarily mean a displacement of nomos by thesis. If the means for the alleviation of poverty are raised according to general rules, government will not have to subject the individual and his property to its discretionary authority and the individual will remain free to pursue his own ends. However, some of our social goals cannot be achieved under nomos but only under thesis. These social goals that cannot be achieved in a system of rules of just conduct are those that we described in the last chapter as social, or distributive, justice. Social justice is the attempt to secure a concrete state of affairs for particular people and this cannot be accomplished with general rules but only with rules that direct particular people to do particular things.[34]

Some political philosophers see law as being an encroachment on liberty because they see law only as thesis or as rules that establish a concrete order by directing particular people to secure particular results. They do not view law as the chief condition of liberty because they are unable to distinguish nomos, which leads to an abstract order, from thesis. And, as we have said, if the distinction between nomos and thesis fades, Hayek believes that thesis will prevail over nomos.

The purpose of Hayek's distinction between nomos and thesis is to exclude the private citizen and his property from the category of means for government ends and to subject government to the same rules as individuals and other organizations. Seen merely in this way, the law does not so much give government power over individuals as limit the power of government over individuals. Thus, law is not an infringement of individual liberty but rather it prevents infringements of liberty. His theory, however, hinges on this distinction between thesis and nomos and on the superiority of nomos over thesis. How valid is this distinction?

Following Hayek, we can say that there is a difference between rules that prohibit killing and stealing, and rules that say that each state must have two senators or that the president is limited to two four-year terms. The distinction here, I think, is rather clear. The first sort of rule limits individual conduct while the second is a rule of organization.

However, the distinction that Hayek draws may be a bit too fine. Is a law that directs individuals to shovel snow off the public sidewalk in the front of their homes thesis or nomos? Is it a valid or invalid use of law? According to this distinction, even taxation could create a theoretical difficulty. Taxation is the compulsory raising of means from private individuals to support government activities, and a particular individual may care little about, or may even be opposed to, some of these activities. However, since tax revenues will provide for some common ends, perhaps we should not make too much of this problem. But there are some other problems. For instance, in principle, Hayek is not opposed to a military draft or, with compensation, the expropriation of landed property (i.e., eminent domain).[35] Yet, these laws extend the power of the government and, to a degree, make the individual and his property a means of the government. Hayek makes no attempt at explaining how either compulsory military service or the expropriation of property can be explained or justified in terms of his distinction between thesis and nomos.

AN EFFECTIVE LEGAL SYSTEM AND A TEST OF JUSTICE

Since we have seen the most important aspect of Hayek's legal thought (the distinction between thesis and nomos), we shall now elaborate on another important element of his legal theory. We shall discuss Hayek's suggestions for improving a legal system and his theory of justice. Though Hayek discusses these two topics separately, they are closely related and we shall therefore consider them under the same heading.

As we pointed out in the previous chapter, and as Hayek ceaselessly emphasizes, rules are necessary because of human ignorance. No one source can know all human ends, and no one source can know all the particular facts upon which civilization is built. Rules "are multi-purpose instruments" in that they allow each person to seek his own end.[36] According to Hayek, it is only because we do not know the future outcome of observing rules that we are able to agree on rules. As an example, Hayek says, mothers "could never agree whose desperately ill child the doctor should attend first"; however, they may well agree that he should "attend the children in some regular order which increased his efficiency."[37]

Though rules of just conduct are largely the product of tradition, a legal order can be improved by human craftsmanship. In attempting to legislate on rules of just conduct, Hayek suggests that we judge rules according to three criteria. Since we cannot know the effects of a rule in each particular case, we must apply the test of universalization to each rule. Rules prohibit certain types of actions and in some cases the results of this prohibition will be beneficial and in other cases it will not be beneficial. Thus, when legislating rules of just conduct we must decide if the benefits of a universal prohibition outweigh the benefits of allowing a particular type of behavior.[38]

Also, since law serves to form and maintain an order of actions, for a system of rules to be effective, particular rules must be "applied to all cases to which they refer" and they must be "adhered to for long periods."[39] The function of an abstract order is to serve unknown ends. The law is concerned with abstract relationships between individuals and thus with long-term and unforeseeable results. If the law is applied selectively, or is seen as important for its short-term results, it will come to serve particular foreseeable results, and this will destroy the rationale for a legal system.

There is another test that Hayek applies to particular laws to judge both if they are just and if they will improve the legal system. This test he alternately refers to as "immanent criticism," the "negative test of universalibility," and "the test of internal consistency."[40]

Though rules are largely the product of tradition, Hayek says that particular rules can be improved by a method of immanent criticism. A legal system is never completely designed, and in order to improve it the whole must be used to judge the part. What Hayek means is that a social environment is an order of actions that is based on a system of rules. In order to improve the legal system, a particular rule can be judged only in terms of its consistency or inconsistency with the entire system of rules and, more important, with the resulting order of actions. A system of law is the product of the collective wisdom of the ages and cannot be challenged all at once. Thus, only one rule at a time can be judged and it can be judged only by "other products of tradition."[41] The main point is not that there is a logical compatibility between different rules but that the rules are conducive to a compatibility of the actions of individuals, that is, the rules prevent conflict. Even two rules that are logically contradictory could be compatible if they achieve consistency in action, and they can do this if they are arranged hierarchically.[42]

Hayek defines justice solely in terms of human conduct. A state of affairs, simply by being desirable or undesirable, is neither just nor unjust. Since Hayek defines justice in terms of human conduct, he concludes that only nomos and not thesis is directly concerned with justice.[43] The purpose of nomos is an abstract order and not concrete results. Therefore, justice, like law, is concerned with methods and not with individual results.[44] In regard to an entire legal system, Hayek means that justice can only be a system of rules that applies to relations between individuals, with the word compatible implicit in the word system and the word abstract implicit in the word rules.

Since Hayek sees justice as a system of rules that applies to relations between individuals, he believes that he has an objective test of justice and that this test consists of "the necessity of commitment to the universal application of the rules laid down, and the endeavour to modify and supplement the existing rules so as to eliminate all conflict between them."[45] This test is a negative test; it will eliminate the unjust, but it will not necessarily assure us of attaining ultimate justice.[46] We can judge the justice or the injustice of a particular rule by its compatibility with an entire system of law. This test gives us an objective criterion by which to judge the justice or injustice of a particular law.

In his discussion of law and justice, Hayek is highly critical of theorists he calls legal positivists, and among theoreticians of positivism he lists Thomas Hobbes, Jeremy Bentham, John Austin, and Hans Kelsen. According to the positivists, all law is created and thus there is no justice other than that legislated by a sovereign. Indeed, Kelsen goes so far as to assert that the Nazi regime was one of law. However, Hayek argues that by postulating that all law is made the positivists mistakenly subsume nomos under thesis and thus entirely miss the point that the very purpose of law is the maintenance of an abstract order that has not been created by any brain. The positivists are then unable to recognize that a particular law can be determined to be just or unjust by its compatibility or incompatibility with an abstract order.[47]

Though in chapter six we shall comment further on Hayek's negative test of injustice, a few comments on it here are in order. This negative test of injustice is supposed to be an advance on his discussion of justice in *The Constitution of Liberty*. In that work, he says that the only criterion we have to discover the justice or injustice of a particular law is whether or not it is a general rule.[48] However, this negative test of injustice could be so difficult to apply that one might legitimately wonder if it is superior to his earlier and more limited test of justice. For example, certain types of laws regulating, say, abortion, or euthanasia, involve several different principles, and it is questionable if the human mind is capable of considering all these principles and all their logical consequences simultaneously, and at the same time judging if these principles and their consequences are compatible with all other rules and the ramifications following from these other rules. A decision involving such a large number of considerations probably will not be much better than a guess, and if we cannot adequately judge whether or not a particular rule is consistent with an entire legal system we seem to be back to judging a law merely by whether or not it is a general rule. However, in Hayek's defense it should be pointed out that he does not say that it is a simple matter to determine if a single rule is compatible with an entire system of rules but only that this is the only way we can judge if a rule is unjust.

THE EARLY AND RECENT LEGAL PHILOSOPHY OF HAYEK

Before bringing this chapter to a conclusion, we shall make a brief excursion into the development of Hayek's legal theory. Though *Law, Legislation and Liberty* differs in certain respects from his earlier works on law, some commentators seem to suggest that there are no significant differences between his early and more recent legal thought, or that if there are dif-

ferences these differences are merely in the nature of a unilin-
ear development of his thought, that is, Hayek's recent thought
is a logical outgrowth, or merely an elaboration, of his earlier
positions.[49] While I do not want to deny that some of the differences between Hayek's positions over the years have been
in the nature of a logical development of his thought, I do wish
to emphasize that some differences exist, and that some of these
differences are more aptly described as changes or reformu-
lations rather than as elaborations.

As we have seen in this chapter, Hayek emphasizes the superiority of common law to a system of statutory law. However, this has not always been the case. In fact, at one time
he preferred a system of statutory law over that of common
law.

> There is some inherent conflict between a system of case law and the
> ideal of the Rule of Law. Since under case law the judge constantly
> creates law, the principle that he merely applies pre-existing rules
> can under that system be approached even less perfectly than where
> the law is codified. And though the much lauded flexibility of the
> common law may have been favourable to the rise of the Rule of Law
> so long as general opinion tended in that direction, the common law
> also shows, I am afraid, less resistance to its decay once that vigi-
> lance is relaxed which alone can keep liberty alive.[50]

Thus, I think that we can say that Hayek has changed his
opinion on the relative merits of common law vis-à-vis statutory law.[51]

Next, in *The Constitution of Liberty*, Hayek argues that for
law to be conducive to liberty it must be nondiscriminatory, it
must apply equally to all. Yet he notes that some laws refer
to only a part of the population (e.g., only a woman "can be
raped or got with child") and that some of these rules are both
desirable and just.[52] Hayek thus runs into a problem: how can
we justify obviously discriminatory law without at the same
time conferring an unjust and arbitrary power on government? Hayek invents a test that he believes justifies some types
of discriminatory law and that yet prevents government from
exercising arbitrary power. This test consists of having a majority inside the group (i.e., the people to be distinguished by

a law), approve of the law and a majority of those outside of the group approve of the law. If a majority of both those inside and outside the group accept the distinction, the law will not be unjust or arbitrary.

Though in *The Constitution of Liberty* Hayek treats this test as though it is of great importance, I doubt if he continues to believe that it is useful.[53] First, he never explains the relationship between this test and his negative test of injustice. If in a particular case there is a conflict in a decision resulting from the application of the two different tests, which one takes precedence? Second, this test has received some rather stinging criticism. According to Hamowy, a majority of blacks and a majority of whites might both be opposed to interracial marriage. But would this make a law prohibiting interracial marriage just?[54] Third, Hayek's test just does not make much sense, not even in regard to the example he gives. If one starts off with the premise that violence and coercion should be prevented (which is Hayek's position), why is it necessary to invent a special justification for a law prohibiting rape? Moreover, suppose a majority of men do not approve of laws against rape, would rape then be just? On a more mundane level, what is the institutional machinery by which we can ascertain whether or not we have the approval of a majority inside all various groups and a majority outside all various groups? Finally, Hayek does not refer to this test in *Law, Legislation and Liberty*, or, so far as I can find, in any of his works published more recently than *The Constitution of Liberty*. For these reasons, I think it is very likely that Hayek has simply discarded this test.

SUMMARY AND CONCLUSION

There are two chief considerations that lead Hayek to conclude that the law is conducive to freedom. The first consideration is that law and government are distinct. Some of the theorists who have criticized Hayek's view that law leads to liberty have a tendency to define law in terms of government. Hans Kelsen says, the rule of law principle does not guarantee the freedom of the individuals subject to the government because it does not refer to the relation between the government and the governed but to a relation within the government, the relation between the law-creating and the law-applying function; its purpose is the conformity of the latter to the former.[55]

Kelsen here defines law in terms of government, or what Hayek calls thesis, that is, instructions emanating from an assembly and directed to an executive.

Herman Finer says:

it is one of Hayek's favorite tricks in oral debate on the theme of the Rule of Law, as we have discussed it, to put this truculent question, which he regards as consternation-making and decisive. "If a majority voted a dictator, say Hitler, into power would that still be the Rule of Law?" Indeed, he puts this question in *The Road to Serfdom*. The answer is Yes; the majority would be right: the Rule of Law would be in operation, if the majority voted him into power. The majority might be unwise, and it might be wicked, but the Rule of Law would prevail. For in a democracy right is what the majority makes it to be.[56]

It seems that Finer's animadversion is also based on an identity of government and law. If "in a democracy right is what the majority makes it to be," it seems to follow that in an oligarchy right is what the few wealthy make it to be and that in a dictatorship right is what a dictator makes it to be. Hayek, however, is able to maintain that the law is a barrier to governmental power by making a distinction between government and law. And surely, the reason why he emphasizes the evolutionary origin of law and the created origin of government is to show that law has an existence that is not only independent of, but prior to, the existence of government. By demonstrating an origin of law that is independent of government, Hayek is able to keep the two definitionally distinct, and he can then maintain that the law prevents certain types of actions, even actions performed by government. If Hayek had postulated that government was the creator of all law, it is difficult to see how he could have argued that an entity's own creation can limit that entity's power. It is more likely that he would be left to conclude that law is whatever a government says it is.

The controversy over the effect of law on the liberty of the individual is at least in part a controversy over definition (i.e., is law distinguishable from government or from acts of government?). Though there are those that reject Hayek's distinction, there are historians of constitutionalism who not only accept Hayek's distinction, but agree with him that this distinction is no longer as sharp as it once was and further agree with him on the consequences of not adequately distinguishing the two.

The particular author I have in mind is Charles Howard McIlwain, whom another well-known historian has referred to as "that most eminent of constitutional historians."[57] McIlwain's position is strikingly similar to Hayek's, and it is astounding that Hayek never mentions this author in regard to what is McIlwain's main argument, though Hayek does cite McIlwain in regard to a large number of peripheral points. To show that Hayek is not alone in his concerns, we shall briefly juxtapose the positions of these two authors. As Hayek borrows the terms thesis and nomos from a previous era to distinguish acts of government from law, and to show that the distinction is no longer as clear as it once was, McIlwain borrows the terms gubernaculum and jurisdictio from a previous era for the same purpose.[58] The king, says McIlwain, was "under no man" and had a supreme power.[59] Yet, the king had a supreme power only in regard to "something which 'pertains to the administration of the realm,'" that is, gubernaculum.[60] In regard to the private citizen, "jurisdictio marked the limits of the king's authority."[61] Judges were "bound by their own oaths to determine the rights of the subject not according to the king's will but according to law."[62] This distinction between gubernaculum and jurisdictio has been "overlooked in modern times" as has "the distinction between an enactment of administrative procedure, on the one hand, and, on the other, a definition of legal right. This distinction is fundamental with

Bracton, but has been forgotten by us."[63] McIlwain says, "the two outstanding features that distinguish the medieval constitution from the modern are, then, the separation of government and jurisdiction, and the difference in legal effect between an administrative order and a definition of legal right."[64]

As Hayek concludes that a lack of distinction between thesis and nomos will cause the destruction of nomos by thesis, McIlwain comes to a similar conclusion in regard to gubernaculum and jurisdictio. "Never in recorded history, I believe, has the individual been in greater danger from government than now, never has jurisdiction been in greater jeopardy from gubernaculum, and never has there been such need that we should clearly see this danger and guard against it."[65] And again like Hayek, though unlike Finer, McIlwain does not define law in terms of government, not even in regard to a democratic state. "Even in a popular state . . . the problem of law versus will remains the most important of all practical problems."[66]

The separation of law and government is the first consideration that leads Hayek to conclude that law is conducive to a state of individual liberty. The second and most important consideration is that there is such an order as a catallaxy. Some observers note that in his exposition of law, Hayek is defending a particular type of economic system.[67] They are quite right. The purpose of law is the creation and maintenance of an abstract order, that is, a catallaxy. Law is a neutral authority because it does not serve any particular ends; since it prohibits interference in the use of means, law serves a multiplicity of ends by allowing each person to decide his own individual ends. If nomos is destroyed, one of two consequences must occur, either civilization will collapse or thesis will have to replace nomos. Thesis can replace nomos as an ordering principle of society only where there is complete agreement on a comprehensive choice of ends or where coercion is a substitute for agreement. The law forms a spontaneous order in which there is not an agreement on ends. Hayek's argument on the positive relationship between law and liberty stands or falls on his theory of the catallaxy.

NOTES

1. Hayek, 1973c, p. 52, Hayek, 1960a, p. 60; Hayek, 1944, p. 82.
2. Hayek, 1973c, pp. 73, 75, 77–78, 82–84.
3. Hayek, 1973c, p. 84.
4. Hayek, 1973c, p. 85.
5. Hayek, 1973c, pp. 67, 90, 112, 114, 117, 126–127; Hayek, 1976e, pp. 44–56.
6. Hayek, 1973c, pp. 107–108, 110, 113; Hayek, 1976e, pp. 3, 35.
7. Hayek, 1973c, p. 95.
8. Hayek, 1973c, p. 94.
9. Hayek, 1973c, p. 86.
10. Hayek, 1973c, p. 101. Also see our discussion in ch. 2 above.
11. Hayek, 1973c, p. 170 n. 10.
12. Hayek, 1979, p. 115; Hayek, 1944, p. 37; Hayek, 1960a, p. 225; Hayek, 1955b, pp. 46–47.
13. Hayek, 1973c, pp. 85–86; Hayek, 1976e, p. 35.
14. Hayek, 1976e, pp. 35–37.
15. Hayek, 1973c, pp. 86–88, 97–98.
16. Hayek, 1973c, pp. 100–101, 104.
17. Hayek, 1973c, p. 123.
18. Hayek, 1973c, pp. 116–118.
19. Hayek, 1973c, p. 88.
20. Hayek, 1973c, p. 91.
21. See Hart, 1961, pp. 49–76. Also McIlwain, 1939, pp. 26–85.
22. Hayek, 1973c, pp. 91–95; Hayek, 1976e, pp. 13, 61; Hayek, 1979, p. 123.
23. Hayek, 1960a, pp. 103, 445 n. 14.
24. Hayek, 1979, pp. 135–136.
25. Hayek, 1960a, p. 206; Hayek, 1973c, pp. 6–7. Also see the discussion of persuasive definitions by Cranston, 1967, pp. 46–62.
26. Hayek, 1973c, pp. 124–125.
27. Hayek, 1973c, pp. 134–135.
28. Hayek, 1973c, pp. 136–137.
29. Hayek, 1973c, pp. 137–138.
30. Hayek, 1976e, p. 142; Hayek, 1960a, pp. 227–230; Hayek, 1955b, p. 48.
31. Davis, 1969, pp. 30–32.
32. Hayek, 1973c, p. 127.
33. Hayek, 1973c, pp. 126–127.
34. Hayek, 1973c, p. 142.

35. Hayek, 1960a, pp. 143, 217, 351, 365, 375; Hayek, 1967b, p. 349; Hayek, 1979, pp. 62–63.

36. Hayek, 1976e, p. 4.

37. Hayek, 1976e, p. 4.

38. Hayek, 1976e, p. 28.

39. Hayek, 1976e, pp. 16, 29.

40. Hayek, 1976e, pp. 24, 27, 40.

41. Hayek, 1976e, p. 25.

42. Hayek, 1976e, p. 24.

43. Hayek, 1976e, p. 33.

44. Hayek, 1976e, pp. 38–39. Hayek sometimes refers to this as commutative justice. See Hayek, 1978c, p. 139.

45. Hayek, 1976e, p. 40.

46. Hayek, 1976e, pp. 40, 43; Hayek, 1967b, p. 168; Hayek, 1978c, p. 139.

47. Hayek, 1976e, pp. 44–56.

48. Hayek, 1960a, p. 210.

49. See Dietze, 1976, p. 110; Barry, 1979, p. 82; and even Hayek, 1979, pp. xii-xiii. However, for an opinion closer to that in the text see Lucas, 1979, p. 160.

50. Hayek, 1955b, p. 19, and also see pp. 33, 36; Hayek, 1960a, p. 198. It appears that the work of Bruno Leoni may have influenced Hayek's train of thought. See Leoni, 1961. Hayek comments on Leoni in Hayek, 1973c, p. 168 n. 35.

51. See remarks by Barry, 1979, p. 88. However, see Shenfield, 1961, p. 60. Also see how Hayek's treatment of John Locke's legal philosophy has changed. Compare Hayek, 1955b, p. 10, with Hayek, 1973c, p. 118.

52. Hayek, 1960a, p. 154.

53. Dietz, 1976, does not mention this test; Barry, 1979, p. 93, does not raise any questions concerning Hayek's continued use of it.

54. Hamowy, 1971, p. 362.

55. Kelsen, 1955, p. 78.

56. Finer, 1963, p. 60.

57. Schlesinger, 1974, p. 401 n. 1.

58. McIlwain, 1947, p. 77. Also see the distinction between "a rule of law and the rule of law" by Goodhart, 1958, pp. 946–947.

59. McIlwain, 1947, p. 111.

60. McIlwain, 1947, p. 82.

61. McIlwain, 1947, p. 118.

62. McIlwain, 1947, p. 86.

63. McIlwain, 1947, p. 82. Also, on p. 79, in regard to the distinc-

tion between gubernaculum and jurisdictio, he says, "the debates in parliament and in Westminster Hall even in the early seventeenth century show plainly that the men of the time, whether unconsciously or intentionally, frequently blur this distinction."

64. McIlwain, 1947, p. 86.

65. McIlwain, 1947, p. 140.

66. McIlwain, 1947, p. 145.

67. See Friedmann, 1972, p. 501; Jones, 1958, pp. 146–147; Raz, 1979, pp. 20–21.

V.

Freedom, Democracy, and Constitutionalism

In his political writings, Hayek emphasizes the desirability of a social order in which each individual is free to use his knowledge for his own purposes. By preventing individuals from coercing each other, government contributes to the preservation of this order. However, since government uses coercion, it is also a threat to individual liberty. Though democratic and constitutional procedures are designed to protect individual freedom, current democratic and constitutional devices for limiting the powers of government have failed. We are, Hayek believes, drifting toward totalitarianism because of the progressive destruction of the market, which is in part the result of contemporary democratic methods that paralyze the price mechanism.[1] Since he perceives a failure in contemporary government, Hayek describes a model constitution that he believes will prevent a government from extirpating the self-generating characteristics of society. In this chapter, we shall present Hayek's constitutional design. However, before presenting this design, we shall first expiscate Hayek's position on the relationship between democracy and freedom and, second, his reasons for viewing contemporary democracies with both disdain and alarm.

DEMOCRACY AND FREEDOM

Hayek considers democracy to be important. However, democracy is a form of government, and like other forms of government it can come in one of two varieties: a limited one or an unlimited one. An unlimited democracy like any other form of unlimited government is inimical to individual freedom. Democracy and liberalism are distinct doctrines. Liberalism concerns the limitation of governmental power; democracy concerns who exercises power, specifically, it designates the majority of citizens as the source of power.[2] For the preservation of individual liberty, the source of power is not as important as the limitation of power.[3] Hayek argues that for an individual to be free there must be a sphere of activities that is independent of government and government must be under law. This is the case even when a government operates according to the principle of majority rule.[4] In the past as political power changed hands from monarchs to democratically elected assemblies, it was thought that since the people had replaced a single ruler as the source of political power it had become unnecessary to limit political power. Like John Stuart Mill, Hayek believes that such a view is mistaken and that with the absence of restrictions on a democratically elected assembly tyranny is as possible as under any type of government.[5] A problem of protecting a minority from the majority remains.[6]

Though democracy is not, like peace, justice, and liberty, an ultimate value, Hayek regards democracy as the best form of limited government for three reasons. First, democracy is a peaceful method of changing political leaders. Second, by allowing a majority of the citizens to change political leaders, it helps to prevent tyranny. Third, democracy increases public awareness and understanding of political issues.[7]

As we have seen, Hayek has three prudential arguments for democratic government. The goal, however, is individual freedom, and democracy is superior to other types of government only insofar as it is consistent with limited government. When a democracy is a government under law there are strong reasons to prefer this type of government to any other type of government. Where a majority of individuals are free to rule in any manner they wish, restrained only by their momentary will, democratic government is inferior to non-democratic government that is under the law.[8]

CRITICISMS OF CONTEMPORARY DEMOCRACY

Though in the abstract, Hayek prefers democratic to non-democratic government, he is opposed to the way in which modern democracies are actually conducted. He criticizes contemporary democracies as lawless, corrupt, weak, and undemocratic.

The first charge in Hayek's four-count indictment against contemporary democracy is omnipotence. By this, Hayek means that democratic assemblies are not under law, in the sense of nomos, in the actions which they undertake and that such assemblies believe that they can settle any matter in any manner they like. Government has become arbitrary in the sense that it does not act according to rules.[9] There are two trends of thought that are largely responsible for this state of affairs.

Besides the doctrine of sovereignty, which we have previously discussed, the second intellectual foundation for legislative omnipotence, according to Hayek, is what M. J. C. Vile calls the formal view of government functions versus the material view.[10] According to Vile, in a book that Hayek often mentions and praises, in late nineteenth- and early twentieth-century France there were highly important discussions concerning the meaning of law and of government functions generally. In 1893, Léon Duguit developed the dichotomy of a formal and a material view of law. The material view of government functions, which according to Duguit is the correct view, believes that government functions must be judged by their content, and the distinguishing characteristic of law is its generality, any act that is not general, despite its source, is ipso facto not law. The formal view of a government function, which Vile attributes to Carré de Malberg, defines a function not by its contents or attributes but by its source. Thus, law is something that emanates from a legislature, and it includes everything that comes from a legislature. A decision on a particular matter even by a legislature, argued Duguit, can be law only in the formal sense (i.e., by coming from a legislature) and it cannot be law in the material sense because it is not a generality. Hayek's complaint that contemporary democracies are lawless traces its origin to this dichotomy of the formal view verses the material view. If the formal view is upheld (which Hayek believes is the case), it is impossible for legislatures to act lawlessly because every act that emanates from a legislature is by definition law. Thus, as the sovereignty of law and the sovereignty of a democratic assembly become identical, a popular assembly becomes omnipotent because it is limited by only its will and not by independent rules of just conduct.[11]

Besides having power that is not limited by law, democratic governments wield this power unjustly, and necessarily so. Hayek's charge that contemporary democratic government is corrupt involves what is often called interest group liberalism, and his argument concerns topics we discussed in chapter three, specifically, social justice and the function of prices. Through the political process, organized groups are able to procure benefits for themselves at the expense of others. In order to obtain office, a politician or political party has to have majority support. A political party can be forced to concede to unjust demands solely because a particular group can withhold its support and prevent it from forming a majority of the voters. Even relatively small groups can act as swing groups and enforce their demands by threatening to prevent the formation of a majority. Since the politician's position depends upon the support of such groups, and, even more important, since a democracy has the power to grant concessions, government necessarily becomes the province of special interests.[12]

Farmers demand parity. Businessmen demand tariffs. Laborers demand the exclusion of the semi-skilled from their trades. They all demand government action to protect their relative incomes, and politicians must accede to these demands if they are to remain in office. Hayek does not mince words in describing these demands and their satisfaction. He describes them as a "corruption," a "bribe," "blackmail," and "vote-buying."[13] These demands are met not because they are just, they are met because certain groups can exercise enough political power to pervert both the political and economic process. As government satisfies the demands of some, still more groups clamor for a government fixed income that is above market value. Others want the same privilege extended to themselves.[14]

The system of incomes determined by political struggle has been more kindly described by others. For instance, Professor David Truman finds that pressure group activity has a beneficial and corrective nature. If it were not for pressure groups, wages, prices, and employment would be set by the market mechanism, and this would lead to such undesirable states as waste and unemployment. In describing the origins of economic associations that operate through government, Truman says,

in the first place, there has been a series of disturbances and dislocations consequent upon the utopian attempt, as [Karl] Polanyi calls it, to set up a completely self-regulating market system. This attempt involved a policy of treating the fictitious factors of land, labor, and capital as if they were real, ignoring the fact that they stood for human beings or influences closely affecting the welfare of humans. Application of this policy inevitably meant suffering and dislocation—unemployment, wide fluctuation in prices, waste, and so forth. These disturbances inevitably produced associations—of owners, of workers, of farmers—operating upon government to mitigate and control the ravages of the system through tariffs, subsidies, wage guarantees, social insurance, and the like.[15]

Truman's analysis does not mean, for example, that a particular group desiring a tariff is justified in demanding any level of taxation on foreign imports it desires or even that any particular tariff is justified. It means only that tariffs are a matter of political barter and that they cannot be ruled out on principle. Tariffs are neither inherently good or bad, but particular tariffs can be good or bad. He sees what he describes as potential groups, overlapping memberships, and acceptance of the rules of the game as potentially preventing an economic association from forcing government to make a tariff that is too high.[16] His analysis suggests that the results of competition between organized groups, for example, over tariffs, will generally be just.

Hayek, of course, rules out tariffs and market intervention in principle. The attempt to describe such intervention as anything but unjust or against the general interest cannot be defended, according to Hayek, on any grounds. Since Hayek's position on this matter is closely related to terrain we have previously covered, we shall merely summarize his reasoning. Pressure groups acting through government to correct the ravages of the market actually destabilize the market and ravage other citizens. When an individual seeks to promote his own end he also promotes an end that is no part of his design, that is, he improves the material condition of the public. When a group acts selfishly it harms the public. The point is that when an individual, or firm, seeks to serve himself he must also serve others by being as productive, or more so, than his competitors. However, the situation is not the same in regard to groups. Groups force governments to use coercive means to prohibit efficiency. The entire point of tariffs is to prevent some from being more efficient than others and the result is that the group benefits and the public suffers.[17]

Hayek, of course, is not alone in thinking that group interests pursued through the political system are harmful to the public. In the previous century, Frédéric Bastiat made the same argument but only more forcefully. In response to all the calls for tariffs to prevent ravages of the market and to aid French manufacturers and workers, Bastiat, assuming the role of a candle manufacturer's association, wrote:

To Messieurs the Members of the Chamber of Deputies

Gentlemen,

. . . We are suffering from the intolerable competition of a foreign rival, placed, it would seem, in a condition so far superior to our own for the production of light, that he absolutely inundates our national market with it at a price fabulously reduced. . . . This rival . . . is no other than the sun.

Bastiat went on to argue that the legislature should "shut up as much as possible all access to natural light," which will "create a demand for artificial light," which will in turn create profits for the manufacturers and high salaries for the workers. He concluded:

Make your choice, but be logical; for as long as you exclude, as you do, iron, corn, foreign fabrics, in proportion as their prices approximate to zero, what inconsistency it would be to admit the light of the sun, the price of which is already at zero during the entire day![18]

Hayek does not stop his analysis at the point of showing that organized interests operating through government are harmful to the public, for there are others (he attributes this view to John Kenneth Galbraith and Gunnar Myrdal) who argue that the present effects of group politics are due to a transitional phase in which all interests are not organized and that once all interests are organized the defects will be remedied.[19] In regard to such an argument, Hayek responds on two levels. First, says Hayek, not all groups can organize. Second, even if all groups could organize, the results of group politics would not be just or efficient.

For the first argument, Hayek directs his readers to the work of Mancur Olson, which, he says, demonstrates that all groups cannot organize.[20] Olson is concerned with the view that as individuals with a common interest are threatened by organized interests the unorganized group organizes to conduct political battle. He argues that individuals with common interests do not and will not, except in special cases, through rational action voluntarily join together to promote their common interest. Before individuals join together to promote a common interest at least one of three conditions must be met: one, the group must be small; two, coercion must be applied; three, special incentives (which he refers to as the by-product theory) must be present.[21]

We shall briefly summarize what Olson means by these three conditions. Though within a small group individuals may band together to promote a common end, rational individuals in a large group will not voluntarily contribute to a common aim because an individual's actions in promoting this end will be imperceptible and he will benefit anyway from the efforts of others. Olson offers some insightful examples involving taxation and inflation.[22]

Olson's second condition, coercion, is discussed mainly in regard to labor unions. Though a large group cannot, by voluntary rational action, be formed to promote a common interest, it can be organized by coercion. Unions usually begin as locals, though, no sooner do unions organize than they are forced to expand. "Market forces work against any organization that operates only in part of a market. Employers often will not be able to survive if they pay higher wages than competing firms."[23] However, since during a strike the amount of labor decreases and the strike breaker's salary increases, an individual has a pecuniary incentive to ignore union policy. How then can a national union survive? Only by coercion. "Compulsory membership and picket lines are therefore of the essence of unionism."[24]

The third way organizations that pursue a common interest can form is according to the by-product theory. According to this theory, organizations that pursue a common interest originate and survive because they provide non-collective, or individual, goods. As an example, Olson cites the American Medical Association (AMA), which he says uses both coercion and non-collective goods or special incentives. Focusing only on the special incentives, the AMA publishes a journal that most doctors purchase and read. It also sells advertising to drug companies, and then, according to one author that Olson cites (Oliver Garceau), grants the AMA seal of approval for their products. The proceeds from the journal and advertisements then go toward supporting a lobbying effort.[25]

Apparently only some groups have these options open to them, for both Olson and Hayek argue that some of the largest and most important groups cannot organize. Among those, according to Olson, who are not organized are migrant farm laborers, white collar workers, consumers, people with an interest in peace (as opposed to those " 'special interests' that may on occasion have an interest in war"), and those who want to prevent inflation and depression. To this list, Hayek adds women and the aged. Hayek and Olson both conclude that individuals who cannot organize will suffer as a result of the efforts of organized interests.[26]

However, suppose the preceding analysis is in error, that is, if all interests could organize, would the result then be a just and efficient social order? Hayek's answer is no. In order to maintain a certain standard of income, the organized groups must be able to control their prices and control the quantity of labor, at least to the degree that they can prevent the influx of new members into their trades. Yet, it is a functioning price system and the freedom of individuals to change occupations that generates a high level of production. Though it may be in the interest of each particular group to control its prices and membership, this is not in the general interest. If the privilege to determine incomes by political means is extended to everyone, the price mechanism will no longer reflect changing circumstances and we shall all suffer from declining production. If this privilege is not extended to all, it cannot in justice be extended to some.[27]

Though these group demands are illegitimate, Hayek believes that interest groups have been successful in achieving privileges partly because they have been able to camouflage the injustice of their acts with the morally high-sounding title of social justice.[28] However, the main problem is not the fact that groups organize but that contemporary democratic government is not government under law and thus can grant privileges to particular groups. For if government was unable to grant privileges, the incentive for people with common economic interests to organize would vanish.[29]

Hayek's third charge against contemporary democratic government is weakness. Hayek argues that if a democracy is not under law it is necessarily a weak government. Any lawless government can confer special benefits on particular segments of the population. What distinguishes a lawless democracy from other types of government is that a lawless democracy must confer special benefits. Since a democratic assembly can do anything, and since its support depends on special interests, those in such an assembly must do as the special interests dictate or cease to be members of such an assembly. This has the effect of making a majority, which is composed of minority groups, extremely powerful and yet "wholly incapable of pursuing a consistent course of action."[30] Government programs are not the result of planning but the result of ad hoc bargaining on particular issues.

Hayek's final charge against contemporary democracy is that

it is not democratic at all. Like some other political theorists, Hayek comes to the conclusion that modern democracy is a system of decision making in which minorities, and not a majority, determine specific government policies. Robert A. Dahl, for instance, further concludes that though in a democracy a majority does not rule on specific policies, a majority does govern in the sense that minority decisions on public policy almost always take place within the values set by a majority of the voters.[31] Hayek, however, argues that contemporary democracies are undemocratic because the majority cannot make the values it agrees on prevail, and, paradoxically, it cannot do so, because the majority is omnipotent.

Before showing how Hayek reaches this conclusion, we shall first explain what Hayek means by the word omnipotent. Though, so far as I can ascertain, Hayek nowhere defines the word, he uses it to mean not subject to law (or rules) and uses it almost interchangeably with the words unlimited, arbitrary, and lawless. Rather than defining the term, Hayek appears merely to describe the word in relation to government. Omnipotence is characterized by the possession of two distinct powers in one set of hands, the power to make (and alter) rules of just conduct and the power to decide on a particular course of action to achieve a concrete objective.[32] In contemporary democracies, a numerical majority is omnipotent because it determines both rules of just conduct and the particular policies of government, and as we shall now see it is because a majority has both powers that it cannot make its principles prevail.

Government is organized to pursue concrete goals, and political parties that contest with each other in the electoral process to control government do so by proposing programs to achieve particular goals. Political parties are composed of organized coalitions that can, by threatening to withdraw their support, force political parties and government to concede special privileges to them. These privileges are not something a majority of people regard as just, but are something a majority will have to concede in order to retain majority status to remain in office and carry out their own programs. If the majority were asked to vote on the principle involved in conceding a particular privilege, it would probably prohibit the concession. But since minority support is necessary to maintain a majority, and more importantly because someone is able to grant privileges, by way of individual concessions, the principles of a majority will not prevail.[33]

Though Hayek thinks that bargaining between organized minorities leads to undemocratic results, he believes that this is necessarily true of only a particular type of bargaining. Though end-independent rules may be able to command widespread approval, specific ends are the result of individual preferences and cannot command widespread approval. In order for the government to achieve certain ends that everyone may not have an interest in, bargaining, in the sense of reciprocity, will probably always be necessary. However, the bargaining must take place under principles approved by a majority and the principles must be unalterable by the bargaining process.[34]

It is the containment of bargaining within principles that will tend to lead to justice, a coherent overall order, and democratic results. It is not the fact that a majority wants something that is an indication of justice. Just as there is a difference between the actions that an individual may be willing to undertake to achieve a particular goal and a rule that circumscribes individual behavior that he may want to see universally observed, there is a difference between what a majority may decide on a particular question and what it might decide on a general principle governing this particular question. In exercising coercion, only the universal application of rules tends to give evidence that the majority has acted justly in particular cases.

Further, if principles do not prevail in a system of rule by minorities on specific policies, it is unlikely that we shall have a coherent overall order of actions. As we pointed out in chapter three, Hayek believes that society is a complex order of highly interconnected human activities. Since organized minorities are concerned with only particular segments of an interrelated series of activities, separate decisions on distinct parts of the social order are unlikely to lead to a consistent pattern of activities, unless the decisions are made according to uniform principles.[35]

In summary, contemporary democracies are undemocratic because the view of the majority on matters of justice and the overall social order cannot prevail, and majority views cannot prevail because it is the same numerical majority that decides both concrete and abstract matters.

Corrupt, lawless, weak, and undemocratic are the charges that Hayek levels against contemporary democracy. These qualities that characterize contemporary democracy, says Hayek, cannot be blamed on the politician, and they are certainly not a necessary consequence of democracy. The problem is not that democratic governments are controlled by majority opinion but rather that they are not restricted to what the people agree on.[36] Though the people can agree on principles or rules that regulate their activities, as you move from the abstract to the concrete opinion becomes more self-interested and agreement necessarily declines. In order for a democracy to be decent government, the procedures that force politicians to promise privileges to organized minorities must be replaced by procedures that will guarantee that majority principles will be upheld. Since the word democracy has become so closely associated with vote buying, Hayek believes that the continued use of that word will merely discredit the ideal of rule by the people. He suggests that we substitute the word *demarchy*, which, he says, can be formed from the Greek words *demos* (people) and *archein* (rule).[37]

Before continuing with our exposition of Hayek's ideas, we shall pause for a moment to comment on several of the topics that we have already presented. Hayek believes that there is general agreement on principles and that if a majority can truly decide issues of principle market intervention will generally be prohibited. However, this does not seem to be necessarily true. If, say, we put a question before the American public concerning the proper role of government in the economy, it is possible that the response will shift according to the way in which the question is asked. For instance, the question "should we subsidize inefficient firms?" might receive a different response than the question "should we help firms raise capital to invest for our future?" Also, there are some questions that may be difficult to answer because they involve several principles. For example, should we prohibit unfair foreign competition? Though I believe Hayek would answer "no," the American public might say "yes" and there is some prima facie plausibility for this answer. Some nations subsidize some of their exports, which is occasionally referred to as "dumping." Those who believe in fair play might well reach the conclusion that our own government should do something, for example, impose tariffs or subsidize domestic firms, in order to prevent foreign producers from benefiting (at the expense of domestic producers) from unfair trade advantages. And if the principle is that no producer should have an artificial advantage over another, there is some difficulty in seeing why the government should not intervene in the market to compensate for these unfair advantages. But yet Hayek's answer, or at least a consistent free market answer (Hayek does not discuss this particular point), would be that we should not, for example, impose a retaliatory tariff, but that we should let the market function. If a foreign nation subsidizes products to sell below cost internationally, the producers of those products in that nation will gain and the country as a whole will lose, that is, the latter will simply be paying for someone else's goods and services. Concerning the nation that the goods are imported into, the domestic producers of those goods will suffer and the country at large will benefit, that is, the consumers will be receiving goods that have, at least in part, been paid for by somebody else. Thus, the free market, without government aid, imposes a discipline on the exporting nation that it can ignore only at its own material disadvantage. However, my conclusion is that it is possible that the public may not understand all the ramifications of the principles behind the market and on occasion it may tolerate intervention in the market.

Before presenting Hayek's remedy for the maladies of contemporary democracy, there are a few problems concerning his diagnosis of the disease. First, is the legislature of the modern democratic state omnipotent, arbitrary, and unjust as he depicts? As we described his position in the previous chapter,

justice is a system of universal rules of just conduct. Almost
by definition any market intervention must be considered unjust. Since market intervention abounds, if one accepts Hayek's definition of justice, then modern legislatures must be
considered to act unjustly. However, at least in the United
States, there are mitigating factors that complicate the analysis and lead to the conclusion that Hayek overstates the case
by saying that a democracy can do anything it wants. The
Congress (or government) of the United States cannot pass ex
post facto laws, bills of attainder, or suspend, except in cases
of rebellion or invasion, the writ of habeas corpus. Perhaps the
legislature is not limited to rules, but because of rights and
procedures guaranteed by the constitution, there are limita-
tions on the power of the legislature.[38]

A second problem involved in Hayek's diagnosis is the explanation of market intervention as caused by organized interests. It would seem that if large groups cannot organize
(without coercion or special incentives), the prima facie case
must always be that government intervention is in behalf of
small groups. Yet, this does not always appear to be the case.
For instance, until recently we have had oil prices regulated
by the government so that they would be below the market
price. But surely there are fewer oil companies than there are
consumers of petroleum. And so with rent control. Just as
surely there are fewer landlords than tenants. Rents, however, are regulated by various regional governments to be below market value. Unless oil consumers or tenants are organized by coercion or special incentives, Hayek's logic would lead
us to believe that if the government is going to regulate rents
or oil prices it will do so for the benefit of the more organiza-
ble group, that is, minimum prices will be established to benefit the smaller group. If these regulations cannot be explained by coercion or special incentives, a theory other than
the one Hayek accepts is necessary to explain market intervention.

Also, there is a problem involved in measuring the actual
strength of groups in the political process. According to Hayek,
an individual's interest is not bound up with a group. Thus,
there is reason to speculate that in an election there may be

a difference between the candidate that an individual supports, and the candidate that his labor union supports, because the individual may take all of his interests into account and his union may take only one of his interests into account. Also, according to Olson, "there is a 'threshold' above which costs and returns influence a person's action, and below which they do not." To many people the cost of voting is insignificant.[39] Thus, though a large number of people like those who have an interest in preventing inflation, depression, high taxes, and war will not organize, they may nevertheless vote in elections because of the low costs involved. If an individual's interest is not tied up with a group, and if those that are unable to organize vote in elections, this must have the effect of diluting a group's strength in an election and also weakening its effect in the legislative process. The strength of the interest group depends ultimately on its ability to deliver its vote as a block and also on the unlikelihood that the non-organized will vote. The extent to which these two factors occur, and thus the extent to which organized interests actually pervert the political process, is an empirical question.

THE CONSEQUENCES OF CONTEMPORARY DEMOCRACY

Since we have considered Hayek's criticisms of contemporary democracy, we shall now give a fuller explanation of why he believes democratic states have developed in the manner we have just described, and, we shall also give a fuller explication of where he believes the further development of democratic institutions, along the lines he inveighs against, will lead.

Hayek believes that unlimited democracy arose, in part, because the same governmental body came to have the distinct powers of controlling government and making law. The lack of structural differentiation between the governmental function and the legislative function ultimately led to the belief that every act of a legislative assembly is law and therefore anything government does is lawful.

Moreover, since the time when assemblies acquired both powers, they have been preoccupied with (and organized along lines to conduct) government. By offering alternative policies to the public, political parties are vital for running government but not for developing law. Since justice is independent of individual and group interests, organized factions have no place in a legislative assembly. It is only where we are interested in particular programs that an assembly organized along party lines is necessary. The reason many of our ancestors were "apprehensive" about assemblies organized along party lines is that they viewed these assemblies as primarily legislative, and not governmental, in nature.[40]

Where will the further development of democratic institutions along these lines lead? Since organized factions demand privileges, and since the powers of government are not limited by law, politicians face an "irresistible pressure" and will likely be forced to organize an increasing amount of society's resources to satisfy their constituents desires.[41] This will push us closer to totalitarianism, or, what is the same thing, tend to make government and society synonymous.[42]

AN IDEAL CONSTITUTION

For a variety of reasons, Hayek sketches a constitution that he believes will preserve individual liberty.[43] Since this sketch is in considerable detail, we shall confine our analysis to the principal elements.

In his study of the American presidency, Richard Neustadt observes that "the constitutional convention of 1787 is supposed to have created a government of 'separated powers.' It did nothing of the sort. Rather, it created a government of separated institutions sharing powers."[44] Hayek believes that an institutional sharing of powers is a defect that afflicts modern constitutions, and his model constitution is an attempt to illustrate the benefits of a strict application of the principle of a separation of powers. Though in modern times a separation of powers has never existed because the same assembly that makes law also directs government, Hayek believes that there are some historical parallels to his constitutional scheme, especially in ancient Athens.[45]

The basic clause of Hayek's constitution will define law and restrict the use of governmental coercion to the application of rules approved of by a majority of the citizens. To effectuate a government limited by law, Hayek's most important institutional arrangement is to have two separate representative bodies with different memberships and elected by different procedures possessing distinct powers: one, the legislative assembly, will make laws or rules of just conduct, while the second, the governmental assembly, will direct the activities of government. The legislative assembly, which, after a similar ancient Greek institution, Hayek occasionally refers to as the nomothetae, will be concerned with nomos or rules of conduct, for example, commercial law, criminal law, the methods of taxation, and health and safety regulations. The governmental assembly will be responsible for organizing the government, deliberating on government ends, and determining appropriate measures to achieve its ends. However, in all its activities, this assembly will be subject to law, and it will be unable to coerce private citizens except in accordance with the law as promulgated by the nomothetae.[46] Thus, presumably, the problem of special interests altering majority supported rules (by individual concessions on particular government programs) will end because the assembly that decides on government programs will be distinct from, and subordinated to, the assembly that makes only general rules of justice.

If the two assemblies represent the same groups of individuals, Hayek believes that the nomothetae and governmental assembly will act in unison and destroy the rationale for the division between the assemblies. Since the nomothetae should represent opinions about justice and not parochial interests, unlike contemporary institutions, it will have to be organized to avoid control by factions and political parties.[47]

Hayek suggests that once in life at the mature age of forty-five citizens elect, either directly or indirectly, a small number of their contemporaries to serve on the legislature. Since by the age of forty-five individuals will have a chance to establish a reputation for themselves, the election by contemporaries will probably lead to a legislature that is composed of competent and respected men and women. To ensure independence of organized groups, Hayek thinks a member of the legislature should be elected for a fifteen-year term, be ineligible for re-election, and have a fixed salary and pension.[48]

Though Hayek's intention is obviously to fill the legislature with high caliber individuals who are independent of pressure groups, the once-in-a-lifetime voting provision, the long-term election provision, and the stricture against reelection seem to undermine two of his three arguments for democracy.[49] The belief that democracy is a peaceful method of change as well as that it tends to prevent tyranny seems to be based on the idea of periodic elections, and in his attempt to insulate the legislature from political pressure, Hayek may have sacrificed two-thirds of his argument for democracy.

Since each age group would one day choose members of the legislature, Hayek believes that semi-private democratic institutions based on age and locality might (spontaneously it seems) develop, and these clubs, or at least one club per locality, should receive public funds. Hayek speculates that individuals would become members of these clubs when they reach the age of eighteen, and members of a particular local club should be allowed to participate in the meetings of other clubs. For a number of reasons, these local clubs would be "a truly democratic link" in the political system.[50] First, they would serve as a potential source of candidates for legislators, or, if a system of indirect elections is chosen, for candidates for delegates to choose legislators. Second, these local clubs would provide a forum for discussion of public issues and offer an education in public affairs. Third, since these clubs would be formed by age groups, they would diminish class and occupational divisions. Lastly, they would furnish a forum for the expression of opinions by individuals not yet represented in the legislature.[51]

In regard to the organization of the governmental assembly, Hayek envisions that it would be like contemporary institutions, that is, members would belong to political parties and be subject to periodical elections, and thus he does not go into detail on the structure of this institution. Two qualifications that he makes concerning the governmental assembly is that whatever method of election is chosen it should not be proportional representation and that the government should not be of the presidential variety. In regard to the first qualification, Hayek does not give much explanation for his position, though if proportional representation is defined as the representation of group interests his reasoning can be gleaned from his criticisms of contemporary democracy and social justice.[52] In regard to his second qualification, Hayek believes that the executive function of government should be carried out by a committee of the majority party in the assembly. By subjecting the President and Congress to separate elections at different times, the United States often has an executive and an assembly that are elected for different reasons and therefore unable to work together. This makes government weak and inefficient.[53]

Also, Hayek believes it is questionable if those who receive government support payments and those who are employed by the government should be allowed to vote for members of the governmental assembly. Since welfare recipients and government employees may have a stronger interest in government expenditures than the ordinary private citizen, Hayek thinks that it may not be wise to allow them to have an authoritative voice in the determination of the level and direction of those expenditures. This potential voting restriction would apply only to the governmental assembly, where particular interests are at stake, and not to the nomothetae, which is concerned with opinions about what is just.[54]

Before commenting on Hayek's institutional division of powers, and then discussing three topics that are related to his constitutional proposals, we shall briefly survey other central government institutions that Hayek discusses. Besides the nomothetae and the governmental assembly, there is a court system (and a distinct body to administer to the personnel and material needs of the courts), a separate court, which he designates the Constitutional Court, to resolve conflicts over areas of specialization by the two assemblies, and a separate body to amend the constitution.[55]

Though Hayek depicts a number of institutions in his model constitution, obviously the most important institutional arrangement is the functional division between a law-making body and a deliberative body, which is based on Hayek's distinction of nomos (rules of conduct) and thesis (government policy or rules of organization). This functional division of powers could be maintained only by an ability to distinguish thesis from nomos and by political methods designed to prevent members of the legislature from representing special interests. Since, in the previous chapter, we commented on the intellectual difficulty of distinguishing thesis from nomos in some cases, we shall here restrict our remarks to Hayek's attempt to ensure that the composition of the legislature does not mirror that of the governmental assembly and that members of the legislature will represent broad, rather than narrow, interests.

There is a dearth of details by Hayek on the election process and this does not assure us that special interests will not control the legislature or that the legislature will not act in unison with the governmental assembly. Since there may be a large number of potential candidates for the legislature, and since there are no organized political parties, how can we prevent the possibility that there would be a splintering of the vote so that individuals who represent only a small faction would be elected? Also, members of both assemblies would appear to have local or regional constituencies which would seem to indicate that they have similar, as well as possibly provincial, outlooks. Moreover, if elections are regional, the potential for swing groups to influence elections seems to be greater than for either local or national elections.[56] Finally, the organization of local youth groups which, in part, Hayek recommends to alleviate class distinctions could have the opposite effect. In some brief remarks, Hayek speculates that localities could become corporations that rent out landed property, and that within the confines of market conditions these corporations will be able to accept or refuse potential residents.[57] If class or occupational status becomes a condition for the admittance of a resident, these local clubs may become an organizational apparatus for class interests.

The first of three special topics concerning Hayek's ideal constitution is the separation of financial powers. Since taxation is a coercive matter, all the rules of taxation must be made by the nomothetae, while the total amount and particular items of expenditure would be determined by the governmental assembly. This division of powers, believes Hayek, will provide a "salutary discipline" on expenditures.[58]

Hayek believes that governments are able to raise and spend as much money as they do because current methods of taxation lead individual citizens to believe that the services they demand will be paid for by someone else. Though Hayek is not completely clear, he appears to be talking about progressive income taxes and some indirect forms of taxation, for example, taxing cigarettes in order to subsidize mass transit. In regard to national government, Hayek appears to believe that taxes should be proportional to income, except where the possibility of a user tax exists, for example, taxing gasoline to pay for roads.[59] Since under Hayek's constitution taxation will have to be under uniform rules (i.e., a proportional income tax) determined by the nomothetae, the representative in the governmental assembly that urges a particular expenditure will know in advance that his constituents will have to pay a predetermined share of the cost and he will not support an expenditure, or total amount of expenditures, his constituents are unwilling to pay for.

The second special topic Hayek discusses is the need for emergency powers by government. Though the central element of Hayek's political philosophy is that governmental power should be limited so that a spontaneous order can fulfill the needs of many individuals, there can be, he believes, instances in which the preservation of this entire order is threatened, for example, by invasion, rebellion, or natural catastrophe, and turning the spontaneous order into an organization is the only effective method of extinguishing the threat. Hayek suggests that the best way to deal with such a threat is that the source declaring an emergency should temporarily renounce its powers. In regard to the constitution he outlines, Hayek says that this means the nomothetae should be the one to declare an emergency and the governmental assembly should receive emergency powers.[60]

The final topic concerning the structural arrangements of Hayek's model constitution is that of federation. As he does throughout most of his discussion of an ideal constitution,

Hayek merely adumbrates his ideas on federalism, and he does not even present his views on federalism in the same setting with his model constitution. Hayek believes that his model constitution is more suitable for federation than are current political arrangements, and only for the sake of brevity, he says, did he describe the model constitution as though it should, or would, be a unitary government.[61]

Hayek's division of political power between central government and local governments is somewhat similar to his division between the nomothetae and the governmental assembly. Presumably because uniform rules are conducive to an abstract order, the legislative power should preferably be national rather than local and regional. However, apart from defense and the enforcement of law, the provision of services should be mainly confined to local or regional governments. To finance its activities, Hayek would allow local government to raise money but only under rules determined by the nomothetae. Thus, law would be the province of the national government, and services would be mainly, though not exclusively, the province of local or regional government.[62]

Hayek has three reasons for making local government the basic source of governmental services. First, it would contribute to a sense of communal spirit. Centralization of government decision making has, believes Hayek, suffocated communal spirit. Decentralization will allow the individual, and not a remote bureaucracy, the opportunity to shape his own surroundings. Second, if funds are raised on a local level and if services are provided on a local level, the benefits and burdens of government activities will tend to balance. Third, government services will be more effectively provided if they are provided on the local or regional level. If local governments must raise their own funds (limited by the rules of the nomothetae) and provide services with these funds, Hayek believes that localities will become like corporations and compete for residents by providing services at costs that would be at least as attractive as those of other communities. Citizens would be able to "vote with their feet for that corporation which offered them the highest benefits compared with the price charged."[63]

CONCLUSION

In this chapter, we have seen Hayek's appraisal of contemporary democracy and we have discussed his proposals for reform. In closing, there is only one further question that we shall consider. Is Hayek attempting to create a weak government? Since Hayek believes that individual liberty is an ultimate end, and that government is the greatest threat to this value, it might be thought that Hayek designs a weak government. Though Hayek limits the coercive powers of government to the application of rules, he does concede to government, and exclusively, the power of coercion, as well as the power to perform non-coercive activities. By placing the coercive powers of government under rules, Hayek would argue that he is giving democratic government more power than it has ever before had, the power to pursue a consistent course of action that is based on principles that are approved of by a majority of the people. But perhaps there is another way of looking at this. According to McIlwain, "a constitutional government will always be a weak government when compared with an arbitrary one."[64] In this sense, Hayek is an exponent of the weak state.

NOTES

1. Hayek, 1973c, pp. 1–2; Hayek, 1978c, p. 162; Hayek, 1979, pp. xiii, 31, 99, 128.

2. Hayek, 1960a, pp. 103–104, 106; Hayek, 1944, p. 70; Hayek, 1978c, p. 143. Schumpeter, 1950, pp. 242, 250, 269, also describes democracy as a method. For a criticism of this type of description see Bachrach, 1967, pp. 10–25.

3. Hayek, 1944, p. 71; Hayek, 1979, p. 128; Hayek, 1978c, p. 154.

4. Hayek, 1960a, p. 109; Hayek, 1979, pp. 100–102; Hayek, 1978c, pp. 157–159.

5. Hayek, 1960a, pp. 107, 444 n. 7; Hayek, 1979, p. 3; Hayek, 1978c, p. 153; Mill, 1956, pp. 4–7.

6. Hayek, 1960a, p. 108.

7. Hayek, 1960a, pp. 107–108; Hayek, 1979, pp. 5, 39, 133, 180 n. 4; Hayek, 1978c, p. 152.

8. Hayek, 1978c, p. 154.

9. Hayek, 1979, pp. 2, 8, 102; Hayek, 1978c, pp. 153–154.

10. For the following discussion, see Vile, 1967, pp. 248–251, 285–286.

11. Hayek, 1979, pp. 2–4, 7–8, 22, 25–26, 33–34, 101–103; Hayek, 1978c, p. 109; Hayek, 1960a, pp. 155–156, 207.

12. Hayek, 1979, pp. 4, 9, 15.

13. Hayek, 1979, pp. 10–11, 13, 32.

14. Hayek, 1979, pp. 12, 150. Also see Lowi, 1969, pp. 87, 292, who describes interest group liberalism as an attempt to universalize privilege.

15. Truman, 1971, p. 61.

16. Truman, 1971, pp. 508–515.

17. Hayek, 1979, see his distinction between labor and enterprise monopoly on p. 83, also see pp. 89–91. Also see Hayek, 1976e, pp. 138–139.

18. Quoted in Heilbroner, 1967, pp. 163–164. For a modern day example of what Bastiat is talking about see Crittenden, 1981, p. 1.

19. Hayek, 1979, p. 93.

20. Hayek, 1979, pp. 96–97, 13.

21. Olson, 1971, pp. 1–2, 120–123, 133.

22. Olson, 1971, pp. 11–14, 33–35, 44, 166.

23. Olson, 1971, p. 67.

24. Olson, 1971, p.71. Also see pp. 70, 72, 74–75, 79, 87.

25. Olson, 1971, pp. 133, 135, 137–141, 148–158.

26. Olson, 1971, pp. 165–167. Hayek, 1979, p. 97. Hayek was apparently so impressed by Olson's book that he had it translated into German. See Olson, 1971, p. viii.

27. Hayek, 1979, pp. 90–94, 142; Olson, 1971, p. 124 n. 52, would agree with this analysis.

28. Hayek, 1979, pp. 10, 95.

29. Hayek, 1979, pp. 95–96, 143–144, 150.

30. Hayek, 1979, pp. 11, 128. Also see Hayek, 1978c, pp. 156–158. On the same point see Lowi, 1969, pp. x, 101, 166, who comes to very similar conclusions.

31. Dahl, 1956, pp. 132–133.

32. Hayek, 1973c, pp. 93, 129–131; Hayek, 1979, pp. 16, 25, 31, 101, 104.

33. Hayek, 1979, pp. 3, 11, 19, 134; Hayek, 1978c, pp. 107–108.

34. Hayek, 1979, pp. 5–8, 14; Hayek, 1978c, p. 109.

35. Hayek, 1979, pp. 17–18.

36. Hayek, 1979, p. 99; Hayek, 1960a, pp. 107, 192.

37. Hayek, 1979, p. 40; Hayek, 1978c, pp. 96–97, 104.

38. Hayek describes American attempts to limit the power of the legislature as partially successful. Hayek, 1979, pp. 21, 26. Also, on procedural rules, see Hayek, 1960a, pp. 218–219.

39. Olson, 1971, p. 164 n. 102.

40. Hayek, 1979, pp. 22–23.

41. Hayek, 1979, p. 128; also, see p. 24.

42. Hayek, 1979, p. 151.

43. Hayek, 1979, pp. xiii, 2, 4, 103, 107–109, 111, 134, 150; Hayek, 1978c, pp. 118, 308; Hayek, 1973c, pp. 1, 3.

44. Neustadt, 1960, p. 33.

45. Hayek, 1979, pp. 111–112; Hayek, 1978c, p. 101; Hayek, 1973c, p. 82. For an explanation of law-making in ancient Athens, see the notes by Ernest Barker in Aristotle, 1958, pp. 128 n. Z, 149 n. FF.

46. Hayek, 1979, pp. 104, 109, 111–112, 115, 119.

47. Hayek, 1979, p. 112.

48. Hayek, 1979, pp. 113–114.

49. See above, p. 94.

50. Hayek, 1979, p. 117.

51. See Hayek, 1979, pp. 117–119.

52. Hayek, 1979, p. 119; Hayek, 1960a, p. 105; Hayek, 1978c, p. 161.

53. Hayek, 1979, pp. 106, 119; Hayek, 1960a, p. 186.

54. Hayek, 1979, pp. 119–120. Like Hayek, John Stuart Mill also argued that welfare recipients should not be allowed to vote, though I do not know of Mill making a similar argument in regard to government employees. See Mill, 1958, pp. 133–135.

55. Hayek, 1979, pp. 38, 107, 120–124.

56. In statewide elections, groups seem to have a disproportionate amount of power. See Price, 1965, p. 33, and also his source. Also, see Koenig, 1975, p. 58, on the effects of changing from the electoral college to a popular nationwide vote.

57. Hayek, 1979, pp. 195–196 n. 14. Also Hayek, 1960a, pp. 351–352.

58. Hayek, 1979, p. 126.

59. Hayek, 1979, pp. 126–127; Hayek, 1960a, pp. 306–324. Hayek, for a great number of reasons, opposes progressive income taxes. He can find only one reason that can justify the progression of income taxes and that is to redress the regressive tendencies of indirect taxes.

60. Hayek, 1979, pp. 124–125, 139–140.

61. For the following discussion of federalism, see Hayek, 1979, pp.

118   A Philosophy of Individual Freedom

45–46, 63, 108–109, 132–133, 145–147, 195–196 n. 14; Hayek, 1978c, p. 162; Hayek, 1960a, pp. 184–185, 351–352; Hayek, 1948, pp. 255–272; Hayek, 1944, pp. 232–238.

62. At least for the United States, where law, civil and criminal, is primarily a state matter, Hayek's theory of federalism conflicts with the practice of federalism. Hayek, however, does note this difference. Hayek, 1979, pp. 132–133.

63. Hayek, 1978c, p. 162.

64. McIlwain, 1947, p. 30.

VI.

A Comprehensive Philosophy of Liberty?

Though Hayek began his academic career as an economist, to a remarkable degree he has taken account of literature throughout the social sciences. Working in the fields of politics, economics, philosophy, and law, he has developed an elaborate statement on the principles of individual freedom.

MARKET ECONOMICS

Although Hayek has delved deeply into the history of political philosophy, it is his study of market economics that forms the center of his philosophy of individual freedom.[1] Starting with the basic assumptions of economics (relatively scarce resources and virtually unlimited human wants), Hayek deduces that freedom is possible only within a market order and he then demonstrates that this order can persist only if individuals are governed by law, that is, abstract rules of conduct. He then argues that abstract rules are unlikely to endure if a single political institution makes both law and public policy. Thus, Hayek's statements on economics, legal philosophy, and the separation of powers are based ultimately on an unraveling of the principles of the market order.

HUMAN IGNORANCE

In his discussion of individual liberty, there are two points that Hayek emphasizes, the ignorance of human beings and the precedence of principle over expediency. As we have seen, Christian Bay unkindly says that Hayek's philosophy is in the spirit of a Callicles and not a Socrates. But perhaps Hayek does have some philosophical kinship to Socrates. As Socrates seems to have aroused some indignation by asking too many difficult questions, Hayek may be unpopular for the same reason. When told that social justice demands a certain level of income for a particular group, or that because society is so complex central direction is necessary, Hayek has a long train of questions that is perhaps too long to suit the impatient reformer. Hayek asks: "What is social justice and how does it differ from justice?" "If a just remuneration should be established for some, what will be the consequences arising from the universal application of the principle involved?" "If some have a right to a particular standard of living, who is under the obligation to provide it?" "If society is complex, how will one source be able to control society without necessarily destroying its complexity?" "Do the proponents of central planning know all the facts that affect each individual's actions?" "Are they wise enough to choose a hierarchy of goals that everyone will accept?" "If there is no agreement on a hierarchy of ends, what will become of individual liberty?" Ignorance of particular facts is a very important aspect of Hayek's political philosophy, and perhaps those who have unfairly criticized him are simply upset because he has challenged the limits of human intelligence.[2] Possibly, this challenge is no more popular to some modern people than it was to some of the ancient Athenians.

PRINCIPLES

Closely related to Hayek's belief in the ignorance of man concerning the particular facts that affect the social order, and just as salient in his political philosophy, is his emphasis on the observance of principles in the exercise of coercion. There are some who put too great an emphasis on political factors in protecting liberty and not enough on the principles limiting coercion by government. For example, in his criticism of Hayek, Professor Tawney implies that things like a market economy are not critical for the preservation of freedom. What is important are political arrangements like representative government.[3] Representative government may well be very important, but Hayek's concern for the preservation of the market and the principles limiting coercion is not misplaced and it is in fact even more important than political arrangements. Concerning the idea of the government owning all the means of production, John Stuart Mill expressed an opinion similar to Hayek's:

If the roads, the railways, the banks, the insurance offices, the great joint-stock companies, the universities, and the public charities were all of them branches of the government; if in addition, the municipal corporations and local boards, with all that now devolves on them, became departments of the central administration; if the employees of all these different enterprises were appointed and paid by the government and looked to the government for every rise in life, not all the freedom of the press and popular constitution of the legislature would make this or any other country free otherwise than in name.[4]

Also, Hayek's description of a state unlimited by principles appears to resemble H. L. A. Hart's description of the game of referee's discretion.[5] Hayek believes that the state cannot use coercion in an ad hoc manner, not even for desirable ends. Hayek emphasizes that the state must be bound by principles in its coercive activities and that once coercion is based on ends, there is no limit to its coercive activities. Unguided by principles, even people of good intentions will be forced progressively to transform the state into something other than they either intend or even foresee. Even in a world in which no one desires to abolish liberty, if principles are not observed the liberal state will gradually be transformed into something quite different.[6]

PROBLEMS

Though Hayek has advanced a serious and very thoughtful argument, there are some problems with it. In his attempt to offer a scientific philosophy based on the market, there are some topics that almost seem to be excluded a priori from the discussion of liberty because they are non-market, for example, freedom of speech, the right to assembly, and the freedom of worship. Problems involving civil liberties receive too little attention from Hayek, and the principles guiding the coercive powers of government in controversies concerning civil liberties are not explicitly discussed at length. If one wants to know the principles to be used in deciding controversies regarding civil liberties, presumably one must rely on his negative test of justice that we described in chapter four.

However, even Hayek's negative test of justice seems to be more applicable to controversies involving economic problems than to controversies arising from civil liberties. This negative test, which involves the universalization of rules, the compatibility of rules with each other, and, most important, compatibility in the order of actions resulting from the rules, can be easily applied to an attempt to establish some sort of economic privilege for a particular group or individual, for example, a tariff. All we would have to do is to show that the universalization of such a measure is not compatible with a market order and that it will lead to the impairment of that order. Relatively speaking, this is not too difficult to do. It is, however, a much more difficult matter to apply this test to controversies respecting civil liberties.

Suppose that, on religious grounds, a man refuses medical treatment for his ill son. The state must choose either to intervene or not to intervene. Which decision would be more compatible with an ongoing order of actions? Would either decision tend to vitiate an ongoing order? In a case like *New York Times Co. v. Sullivan*, should the court allow a suit for libel brought by a public official to proceed by the same standards as if brought by a private citizen, or in the interests of a free press must actual malice be proved?[7] Which decision would be more compatible with an ongoing order of actions? Would either decision tend to destroy an ongoing order? Hayek does not adequately take up dilemmas arising from civil liberties, and his negative test of justice is not as efficacious in deciding civil matters as in deciding economic matters. Regarding the former, Hayek seems merely to adopt the position that no right is absolute, and he appears over-sanguine in the belief that

controversies involving civil liberties will be brought to a sat-
isfactory conclusion in an evolutionary process.[8].

Besides giving too little attention to problems regarding civil
liberties, Hayek somewhat surprisingly does not much discuss
the related ideas of resistance, rebellion, or revolution. Since
Hayek's ideal is a condition of individual liberty and a government limited by law, one might expect a detailed discussion of
how the individual may morally respond to a government that
is not limited by law. But as Gottfried Dietze says,

Hayek mentions revolutions against regimes in which power and
abuses of power were more obvious than authority, such as the revolutions against Charles I and Louis XVI. Yet he does not seem to
come out with a plain statement proposing a right of revolution, although he seems to be sympathetic to such revolutions.[9]

Hayek says that citizens owe an allegiance to government so
long as government ensures the foundations of a self-generating order.[10] But this statement does not say all that much.
What is meant by sustaining the foundations of a self-generating order? Is it a matter of degree? And if and when citizens
no longer owe allegiance to government, are their responses
limited merely to passive resistance or are they morally correct in using violent means, though these may harm innocent
parties, to dispose of a tyrannous regime? Since there cur-
rently are governments that hardly seem to be limited by law,
the topic of resistance, or revolution, would appear to be of more
than merely theoretical interest, yet Hayek does not much
discuss the concept.

The final topic of discussion is Hayek's theory of collective
goods, or the position he takes on the provision of services by
government with revenue raised by compulsory taxation. Hayek
argues that he is not opposed to services being rendered by
government; what he is opposed to is government intervention into the economy that distorts, or makes inoperable, the
market mechanism. Even with a government that supplies a
great many services a condition of individual liberty will prevail, as long as the market mechanism is not distorted.[11] Yet,

Hayek's own theory of government economic activity may not be entirely consistent, and his principles may not limit coercion as much as he would like.

Over the years, Hayek has advanced the principle of reciprocity to justify the expenditure of tax dollars for particular goods and services that may benefit some individuals more than others.[12] To justify the expenditure of public funds for these services, Hayek suggests that we view the public treasury as a common pool of resources to which each contributes according to uniform principles in the expectation that each will receive as much or more in the way of services than each contributes. Thus, the provision of services that benefit some people more than others can be viewed as a type of exchange. I agree to contribute money to the treasury which will be used, in part, to finance some services that will not benefit me as much as you, on the condition that you also contribute to the treasury knowing that you will be contributing funds for some services that will benefit me more than you. Such a system is just if each of us can expect to get as much, or more, out of this common pool as we contribute. But Hayek does not explain how we are to ensure that there is a just proportion between what we pay and what we receive. Furthermore, Hayek also takes the position that even if a particular good is produced by government, if it is also produced privately one should be allowed to procure it from this private source and in fact ought to receive a refund of "any taxes raised for these purposes."[13] This last consideration seems to preclude the principle of reciprocity. How can each of us contribute to a common pool on the basis of reciprocity, if when it is to one's advantage to remove his contribution he can do so?

Some goods, says Hayek, can be provided only if the funds are raised by taxation, however, government is not confined to producing merely these goods. Government can produce any number of goods and services provided:

(1) government does not claim a monopoly and new methods of rendering services through the market (for example, in some now covered by social insurance) are not prevented;

(2) the means are raised by taxation on uniform principles and taxation is not used as an instrument for the redistribution of income; and,

(3) the wants satisfied are collective wants of the community as a whole and not merely collective wants of particular groups.[14]

Hayek often writes as if there are only two legitimate conditions for the provision of government services. The first is that a government agency simply acts as one other firm in the competitive process, that is, it simply produces and sells under the same conditions as a private firm.[15] If the problem of raising the initial capital is solved, there is no reason to believe that government services of this sort would necessarily be inconsistent with Hayek's position.[16]

The second condition for the provision of goods is that they are truly public goods, that is, the goods cannot be provided by the market because they cannot be confined to those willing to pay for them. If they are to be provided at all, they must be financed by compulsory taxation. Among such goods and services are roads (though not long distance roads), police, and defense.[17]

It seems, though, that there is a third type of governmental service that Hayek also accepts as legitimate and that it is redistributive in nature. Since Hayek is not opposed to public support for the indigent,[18] and public financing of education,[19] it is difficult to understand his proviso against taxation as a redistributive instrument. The purpose of financing education is not to provide a service that the market cannot provide (I assume the market can supply this good to some), but to supply a service to someone who cannot afford it. Is this type of service inconsistent with Hayek's position? It is certainly highly inconsistent with his proviso against redistribution.[20] But since Hayek approves of this type of service, he cannot be opposed in principle to taxation for redistributive purposes, but rather he must, to be consistent, mean that redistribution can only be according to universal rules.[21] This may lead to some conclusions that Hayek would not approve of.

We shall now argue that by confining coercion to rules, even to rules that lead to an order of actions, Hayek may not be sufficiently limiting coercion, and that, theoretically if not practically, we can establish within his market order a minimal socialist state. To maintain Hayek's market, we shall assume that the government does not own the means of production and that the government's coercive activities are limited by rules. Even within these conditions, the theoretical possibility exists that a state can arise which guides the factors of production and redistributes income.

By definition, intervention is an arbitrary act of coercion and therefore rules that provide for coercion are not interventionist. Thus, we can accept such measures as taxation, compulsory insurance (e.g., old age or medical insurance),[22] and even a voucher system for education (which system Hayek believes has far more uses than merely education) because they can be applied according to general rules and do not incapacitate the market mechanism.[23]

Imagine that a monarch sees that some of his citizens are ill-fed while others are purchasing luxury goods. The monarch believes that any system of production which provides for frivolous wants while there are still some who have not completely satisfied their basic needs is seriously defective. He strongly desires to intervene in the economic process on an ad hoc basis so that he can shift production from luxuries to the basic necessities. Yet, the people in this society have been reared according to the principle that coercion can be applied only according to uniform rules, and even the people he most desires to help would be appalled at the neglect of this principle. He cannot infringe this rule without losing the allegiance of his subjects. Can our monarch possibly correct the flaws of the market without infringing this principle? Theoretically, the answer is yes. Though the principle of coercion limited by rules will undoubtedly hinder his ability, he can nevertheless still redistribute income and at least partially determine the uses for the factors of production. By a high rate of uniform taxation, he can confine the market order to a very small sphere, and outside this order he can distribute vouchers to each member of his community for specified purchases, for example, for food, for clothing, for shelter, perhaps for medical care, transportation, education, or even periodicals. Through such a redistributive program, he can have a say in the production and distribution of goods and services. And he can do all this without government intervention (i.e., merely by using general rules), or the government ownership of the means of production, and within the principles that some describe as laissez-faire. Such an ambitious program may severely limit individual freedom, and it may not turn out to be in the long-range interest of even the poorest in the community. But in principle, such a socialist, or at least socialistic, state can be created.

With uniform taxation, the creation of a minimal socialist state within Hayekian principles is indeed highly unlikely. Certainly, it is even more unlikely in a democracy, where the legislature is subject to reelection, than in an authoritarian state. Yet, as Hayek says, a liberal state need not be a democratic one. And in principle, there is nothing to prevent the state from taxing individuals at high, but uniform, rates and redistributing the revenue in a way that does not incapacitate the market mechanism.

Would Hayek approve of such a state? Hardly. Though he tells us that in principle his state is not incompatible with a wide range of government services, he does express concern that if the government controls a certain amount of resources, indirectly it will control the economy.[24] Prudentially, he recommends that state activities be kept within narrow limits.[25] And in one passage, he complains of the paternalistic power of government that allows it to redistribute income to individuals in forms and amounts it believes they need.[26] Yet, his principles do not seem to preclude such actions.

If I am right that a minimal socialist state is compatible with Hayek's principles, this raises some interesting theoretical problems for Hayek. Suppose we juxtapose two states, the first is the minimal socialist state which has high redistribution, high rates of taxation, and absolutely no intervention. The second state, the interventionist state, has little redistribution, very low rates of taxation, and a very mild tendency to interfere with the market mechanism. At any one point in time, which state has more freedom? According to Hayekian principles, the minimal socialist state has more freedom. There is no arbitrary coercion, that is, there is no coercion that is not based on rules, in the minimal socialist state, though there is some in the mildly interventionist state. Thus, practically by definition, the first has more freedom than the second. However, this will not do. Hayek has focused too much on the type of coercion and not enough on the degree of coercion. The mildly interventionist state may have more coercion of a particular type, that is, arbitrary, than the minimal socialist state, but if we could measure the amount of coercion in each state we cannot rule out a priori the possibility that the individual in the minimal socialist state is coerced to a higher degree than the individual in the interventionist state. Thus, a country with an unfettered market mechanism is not necessarily superior, in terms of freedom, to a country with a somewhat fettered market mechanism. And freedom then is not merely the product of a functioning market. The degree, as well as the type, of coercion must also be limited to secure a condition of liberty.

There is another interesting theoretical difficulty arising from this line of reasoning. If I am right that the mildly interventionist state can at any point in time have more freedom than the minimal socialist state, we have set the stage for a conflict between freedom and justice. For Hayek, the minimal socialist state would be a just state. The rules of just conduct would be operative, and by assumption the government would be confined by these rules. On the other hand, the mildly interventionist state is not just, or at least not as just as the minimal socialist state. By definition, the mildly interventionist state occasionally elides the rules of just conduct and applies ad hoc coercion. Which is the more desirable state? The state possessing the higher degree of freedom or the state possessing the higher degree of justice?

CONCLUSION

Has Hayek made a comprehensive statement of the principles of a liberal social order? He has certainly succeeded in demonstrating the importance of a market order for the preservation of individual liberty. Yet it is not quite comprehensive. There are some principles that do not revolve around the market, and even after a market is established, the problem of limiting coercion remains.

NOTES

1. Hayek intends his political philosophy to be a scientific statement. Hayek, 1973c, pp. 5–6; Hayek, 1967b, pp. 258–259.

2. If men were omniscient and in complete agreement on ends, there would be little case, says Hayek, for freedom. Hayek, 1967b, pp. 170–171, 257–258; Hayek, 1960a, pp. 29, 66, 97; Hayek, 1976e, p. 8.

3. Tawney, 1953, p. 98.

4. Mill, 1956, p. 135.

5. Hart, 1961, pp. 138–142.

6. On the idea of expediency leading to an illiberal state, see Vile, 1967, pp. 11, 237–238, 286.

7. New York Times Co. v. Sullivan, 376 U.S. 254, 1964.

8. Hayek, 1979, pp. 110–111.

9. Dietz, 1976, p. 141. He bases his remarks on Hayek, 1960a, pp. 164, 194–195.

10. Hayek, 1978c, p. 78.

11. Hayek, 1944, pp. 37, 132; Hayek, 1960a, pp. 222, 227–228, 231, 303; Hayek, 1978c, pp. 92, 111, 306; Hayek, 1976e, p. 139; Hayek, 1979, pp. 41, 53.

12. Hayek, 1960a, p. 144; Hayek, 1973c, pp. 139–140; Hayek, 1976e, pp. 6–7; Hayek, 1979, p. 45.

13. Hayek, 1979, p. 147.

14. Hayek, 1978c, p. 111.

15. Hayek, 1960a, pp. 223–224; Hayek, 1979, pp. 56–59.

16. Presumably the initial capital cannot come from tax revenues because then government would not be competing on the same terms. However, at least theoretically the money could come from gifts or bequeathals. See the discussion of subsidies in Hayek, 1960a, p. 224.

17. Hayek, 1944, pp. 38–39; Hayek, 1960a, pp. 222, 375; Hayek, 1967b, p. 165; Hayek, 1978c, pp. 144–145; Hayek, 1973c, p. 139; Hayek, 1976e, pp. 6–7; Hayek, 1979, pp. 41–42, 44, 139.

18. However, Hayek does not always give the same reason for supporting such measures. See Hayek, 1944, pp. 120–121, 210; Hayek,

1960a, pp. 257, 285, 303; Hayek, 1967b, p. 175; Hayek, 1978c, p. 92; Hayek, 1976e, p. 87; Hayek, 1979, pp. 55, 143.

19. Hayek, 1960a, pp. 223, 376–390; Hayek, 1979, pp. 46, 60–61.

20. Someone might object that public support of education is not really intended to be redistributive, but rather that education has neighborhood benefits, and public support is justified to make those who benefit by it pay for it. Though in part Hayek bases his support for education on neighborhood effects, he does not do so entirely, and I am not sure that public support of this service can be adequately founded solely on neighborhood effects. If, e.g., the case for education is founded solely on the argument that in a democracy public support for education is justified because the people select their leaders, then one would have to conclude that in a non-democratic state, even a liberal one, public support for education is not justified.

21. Hayek, 1955b, p. 46; Hayek, 1960a, p. 221; Hayek, 1978c, p. 144; Hayek, 1976e, p. 129. Hayek, 1979, pp. 5, 109.

22. Hayek, 1960a, pp. 286, 298. Hayek bases the legitimate use of compulsory insurance on neighborhood effects. However, I am not sure that within his principles he needs to do this. And at any rate, other liberal theorists would not be quite as willing to justify compulsory insurance on the grounds of neighborhood effects. See Friedman, 1962, pp. 187–188.

23. Hayek, 1979, p. 46.

24. Hayek, 1944, p. 61.

25. Hayek, 1960a, p. 224.

26. Hayek, 1960a, pp. 260–261. Here though, Hayek is complaining mainly about an arbitrary paternalistic power.

Bibliography

PUBLICATIONS BY F. A. HAYEK

Monetary Theory and the Trade Cycle. London: Jonathan Cape, 1933a.

"The Trend of Economic Thinking." *Economica* 13, 1933b.

The Collected Works of Carl Menger. Introduction to vol. 1 by F. A. Hayek. London: London School of Economics and Political Science, 1934.

Collectivist Economic Planning. F. A. Hayek, ed. London: George Routledge and Sons, 1935a.

Brutzkus, Boris. *Economic Planning in Soviet Russia.* F. A. Hayek, ed. London: George Routledge and Sons, 1935b.

"The Nature and History of the Problem." In F. A. Hayek, ed., *Collectivist Economic Planning.* London: George Routledge and Sons, 1935c (also in 1948).

"The Present State of the Debate." In F. A. Hayek, ed., *Collectivist Economic Planning.* London: George Routledge and Sons, 1935d (also in 1948).

Prices and Production. London: George Routledge and Sons, 1935e.

Thornton, Henry. *An Enquiry into the Nature and Effects of the Paper Credit of Great Britain.* F. A. Hayek, ed. New York: Farrar and Rinehart, 1936.

"Economics and Knowledge." *Economica.* N.s.4, 1937a (also in 1948).

Monetary Nationalism and International Stability. New York: Longmans, Green and Co., 1937b.

"The Economic Conditions of Interstate Federalism." *New Commonwealth Quarterly,* 5, no. 2, September 1939a (also in 1948).

"The Economy of Capital." *The Banker* (London), 52, October 1939b.

"Freedom and the Economic System." In Harry D. Gideonse, ed., *Public Policy Pamphlet No. 29*. Chicago: The University of Chicago Press, 1939c.

"Pricing v. Rationing." *The Banker*. (London), 51, September, 1939d.

Profits, Interest and Investment. London: George Routledge and Sons, 1939e.

"Socialist Calculation: The Competitive Solution." *Economica*, 7, no. 26, 1940 (also in 1948).

"Planning, Science and Freedom." *Nature*, 148, November 15, 1941a.

The Pure Theory of Capital. Chicago: The University of Chicago Press, 1941b.

"The Ricardo Effect." *Economica*, 9, no. 34, 1942 (also in 1948).

"A Commodity Reserve Currency." *Economic Journal*, 53, no. 210, 1943a (also in 1948).

"The Facts of the Social Sciences." *Ethics*, 54, no. 1, October, 1943b (also in 1948).

The Road to Serfdom. Chicago and London: The University of Chicago Press and Routledge & Kegan Paul, 1944.

"Nationalities and States in Central Europe." *Central European Trade Review*, March, 1945a.

"The Uses of Knowledge in Society." *American Economic Review*, 35, no. 4, September, 1945b (also in 1948).

Individualism: True and False. Dublin: Hodges, Figgis and Co., 1946 (also in 1948).

Individualism and Economic Order. Chicago and London: The University of Chicago Press and Routledge & Kegan Paul, 1948.

"The Economics of Development Charges." *The Financial Times*, April 26, 27, 28, 1949a (also in 1967b).

"The Intellectuals and Socialism." *The University of Chicago Law Review*, 16, no. 3, Spring, 1949b (also in 1967b).

"Economics." *Chambers Encyclopedia*, vol. 4. New York: Oxford University Press, 1950a.

"Full Employment, Planning and Inflation." *Institute of Public Affairs Review*. (Melbourne), 4 1950b (also in 1967b).

"Comments on the Economics and Politics of the Modern Corporation." *Conference on Corporation Law and Finance*. Conference Series no. 8. Chicago: The University of Chicago Law School, December, 1951a.

John Stuart Mill and Harriet Taylor. Chicago: The University of Chicago Press, 1951b.

"The Transmission of the Ideals of Economic Freedom." *The Owl* (London), 1951c (also in 1967b).

The Counter Revolution of Science. Glencoe, Ill.: The Free Press, 1952a.

The Sensory Order. Chicago: The University of Chicago Press, 1952b.

Capitalism and the Historians. F. A. Hayek, ed. London: Routledge & Kegan Paul, 1954a.

"History and Politics." In F. A. Hayek, ed., *Capitalism and the Historians.* London: Routledge & Kegan Paul, 1954b (also in 1967b).

"Degrees of Explanation." *British Journal for the Philosophy of Science,* 6, 1955a (also in 1967b).

The Political Ideal of the Rule of Law. Cairo: The National Bank of Egypt, 1955b.

"Toward a Theory of Economic Growth." *National Policy for Economic Welfare at Home and Abroad.* Garden City, N.Y.: Doubleday, 1955c.

"The Dilemma Of Specialization." In Leonard D. White, ed., *The State of the Social Sciences.* Chicago: The University of Chicago Press, 1956a (also in 1967b).

"Reconsideration of Progressive Taxation." In Mary Sennholz, ed., *On Freedom and Free Enterprise.* Princeton: van Nostrand, 1956b.

"The Creative Powers of a Free Civilization." In Felix Morley, ed., *Essays on Individuality.* Philadelphia: University of Pennsylvania Press, 1958a.

"Freedom, Reason and Tradition." *Ethics,* 68, no. 4, July, 1958b.

"Inflation Resulting from the Downward Inflexibility of Wages." In Committee for Economic Development, ed., *Problems of United States Economic Development,* vol. 1. New York: 1958c.

"Unions, Inflation and Profits." In Philip D. Bradley, ed., *The Public Stake in Union Power.* Charlottesville, Va.: University of Virginia Press, 1959 (also in 1967b).

The Constitution of Liberty. Chicago and London: The University of Chicago Press and Routledge & Kegan Paul, 1960a.

"The Corporation in a Democratic Society: In Whose Interest Ought It To and Will It Be Run." In M. Anshen and G. L. Bach, eds., *Management and Corporations 1958.* New York: McGraw-Hill, 1960b (also in 1967b).

"The Social Environment." In Ben H. Bagdikian, ed., *Man's Contracting World in an Expanding Universe.* Providence: Brown University, 1960c.

"The Non Sequitur of the 'Dependence Effect.'" *The Southern Economic Journal,* 27, no. 4, April, 1961 (also in 1967b).

"The Moral Element in Free Enterprise." In The National Association of Manufacturers, ed., *The Spiritual and Moral Significance of Free Enterprise.* New York: 1962a (also in 1967b).

"Rules, Perception and Intelligibility." *Proceedings of the British Academy*, 48, 1962b (also in 1967b).

"The Uses of 'Gresham's Law' as an Illustration of 'Historical Theory.'" *History and Theory*, 1, 1962c (also in 1967b).

Collected Works of John Stuart Mill. Introduction to vol. 12 by F. A. Hayek. Francis E. Mineka, ed. Toronto: University of Toronto Press, 1963a.

"The Legal and Political Philosophy of David Hume." *Il Politico*, 28, no.4, 1963b (also in 1967b).

"Kinds of Order in Society." *New Individualist Review*, 3, no. 2, 1964a.

"The Theory of Complex Phenomena." In M. Bunge, ed., *The Critical Approach to Science and Philosophy*. New York: The Free Press, 1964b (also in 1967b).

"Kinds of Rationalism." *The Economic Studies Quarterly* (Tokyo), 15, no. 3, 1965 (also in 1967b).

"Dr. Bernard Mandeville." *Proceedings of the British Academy*, 52, 1966a (also in 1978c).

"The Misconception of Human Rights as Positive Claims." *Farmand*, Anniversary Issue, 1966b.

"Personal Recollections of Keynes and the 'Keynesian Revolution.'" *Oriental Economist* (Tokyo), 34 January 1966c (also in 1978c).

"The Principles of a Liberal Social Order." *Il Politico*, 31, December 1966d (also in 1967b).

"The Constitution of a Liberal State." *Il Politico*, 32, 1967a (also in 1978c).

Studies in Philosophy, Politics and Economics. Chicago and London: The University of Chicago Press and Routledge & Kegan Paul, 1967b.

The Confusion of Language in Political Thought. London: The Institute of Economic Affairs, 1968a (also in 1978c).

"Economic Thought, vi: The Austrian School." *International Encyclopedia of the Social Sciences,* vol. 4. New York: 1968b.

"Menger, Carl." *International Encyclopedia of the Social Sciences*, vol. 10. New York: 1968c.

"A Self-Generating Order for Society." In John Nef, ed., *Towards a World Community*. Hague: W. Junk, 1968d.

"The Primacy of the Abstract." In A. Koestler and J. R. Smythies, eds., *Beyond Reductionism*. New York: Macmillan Co., 1969a (also in 1978c).

"Three Elucidations of the Ricardo Effect." *Journal of Political Economy*, 77, no. 2, 1969b (also in 1978c).

"Nature v. Nurture Once Again." *Encounter*, 36, no. 2, February 1971a (also in 1978c).

"Principles or Expediency." *Towards Liberty*, vol. 1. Menlo Park, Calif.: Institute for Humane Studies, 1971b.

A Tiger by the Tail. London: The Institute of Economic Affairs, 1972a.

Verdict on Rent Control. London: The Institute of Economic Affairs, 1972b.

Economic Freedom and Representative Government. London: The Institute of Economic Affairs, 1973a (also in 1978c).

"The Place of Menger's Grundsätze in the History of Economic Thought." In J. R. Hicks and W. Weber, eds., *Carl Menger and the Austrian School of Economics*. Oxford: Clarendon Press, 1973b (also in 1978c).

"Rules and Order." *Law, Legislation and Liberty*, vol. 1. Chicago and London: The University of Chicago Press and Routledge & Kegan Paul, 1973c.

Full Employment at Any Price? London: The Institute of Economic Affairs, 1975a.

"Two Types of Mind." *Encounter*, 45, September, 1975b (also in 1978c).

"Adam Smith's Message in Today's Language." *Daily Telegraph* (London), March 9, 1976a (also in 1978c).

Choice in Currency. London: The Institute of Economic Affairs, 1976b (also in 1978c).

Denationalization of Money. London: The Institute of Economic Affairs, 1976c.

"Institutions May Fail, but Democracy Survives." Interview. *U.S. News and World Report*, March 8, 1976d.

"The Mirage of Social Justice." *Law, Legislation and Liberty*, vol. 2. Chicago and London: The University of Chicago Press and Routledge & Kegan Paul, 1976e.

"The New Confusion about Planning." *The Morgan Guaranty Survey*. New York, January, 1976f (also in 1978c).

"Is There a Case for Private Property?" Interview. *Firing Line*. Columbia, South Carolina: Southern Educational Communications Association, 1977.

Denationalization of Money. 2nd ed., revised and enlarged. London: The Institute of Economic Affairs, 1978a.

"The Miscarriage of the Democratic Ideal." *Encounter*, March, 1978b.

New Studies in Philosophy, Politics, Economics and the History of Ideas. Chicago and London: The University of Chicago Press and Routledge & Kegan Paul, 1978c.

"The Political Order of a Free People." *Law, Legislation and Liberty*, vol. 3. Chicago and London: The University of Chicago Press and Routledge & Kegan Paul, 1979.

Law, Legislation and Liberty, in 3 vols. "Rules and Order", vol. 1, 1973c. "The Mirage of Social Justice", vol. 2, 1976e. "The Political Order of a Free People", vol. 3, 1979. Chicago and London: The University of Chicago Press and Routledge & Kegan Paul.

1980s Unemployment and the Unions. London: The Institute of Economic Affairs, 1980.

SECONDARY SOURCES

Aristotle. *Politics*. Translated by Ernest Barker. New York: Oxford University Press, 1958.

Bachrach, Peter. *The Theory of Democratic Elitism*. Boston: Little, Brown and Company, 1967.

Barry, Norman P. *Hayek's Social and Economic Philosophy*. London: The Macmillan Press, 1979.

Bay, Christian. "Hayek's Liberalism: The Constitution of Perpetual Privilege." *The Political Science Reviewer*. Fall, 1971.

Berlin, Isaiah. *Four Essays on Liberty*. New York: Oxford University Press, 1970.

Brecht, Arnold. *Political Theory*. Princeton: Princeton University Press, 1959.

Cranston, Maurice. *Freedom*. London: Longmans, Green and Co., 1967.

Crittenden, Ann. "Growers' Power in Marketing under Attack." *New York Times*. March 25, 1981.

Cunningham, Robert L., ed., *Liberty and the Rule of Law*. College Station: Texas A & M University Press, 1979.

Dahl, Robert. *A Preface to Democratic Theory*. Chicago: The University of Chicago Press, 1956.

Dahrendorf, Ralf. *Essays in the Theory of Society*. Stanford: Stanford University Press, 1968.

Davis, Kenneth Culp. *Discretionary Justice*. Baton Rouge: Louisiana State University Press, 1969.

de Crespigny, Anthony. "F. A. Hayek, Freedom for Progress." In Anthony de Crespigny and Kenneth Minogue, eds., *Contemporary Political Philosophers*. New York: Dodd, Mead and Company, 1975.

Dietze, Gottfried. "Hayek on the Rule of Law." In Fritz Machlup, ed., *Essays on Hayek*. New York: New York University Press, 1976.

Finer, Herman. *The Road to Reaction*. Chicago: Encounter Paperback, 1963.

Friedman, Milton. *Capitalism and Freedom*. Chicago: The University of Chicago Press, 1962.

Friedmann, Wolfgang. *Law in a Changing Society*. Baltimore: Penguin Books, 1972.

Goodhart, Arthur L. "The Rule of Law and Absolute Sovereignty." *University of Pennsylvania Law Review*, 106, no. 7, May, 1958.

Gwyn, W. B. *The Meaning of the Separation of Powers*. New Orleans: Tulane Studies in Political Science, vol. 9, 1965.

Hamowy, Ronald. "Hayek's Concept of Freedom: A Critique." *New Individualist Review*, April, 1961.

————. "Freedom and the Rule of Law in F. A. Hayek." *Il Politico*, 36, 1971.

Hart, H. L. A. *The Concept of Law*. Oxford: Oxford University Press, 1961.

Heilbroner, Robert L. *The Worldly Philosophers*. New York: Simon and Schuster, 1967.

Hume, David. "An Inquiry Concerning the Principles of Morals." In Henry D. Aiken, ed., *Hume's Moral and Political Philosophy*. New York: Hafner Publishing Co., 1972.

Jones, Harry W. "The Rule of Law and the Welfare State." *Columbia Law Review*, 58, no. 2, February, 1958.

Kelsen, Hans. "Foundations of Democracy." Part 2. *Ethics*, 46, no. 1, October, 1955.

Koenig, Louis. *The Chief Executive*. New York: Harcourt Brace Jovanovich, 1975.

Kristol, Irving. *On the Democratic Idea in America*. New York: Harper and Row, 1972.

Lange, Oskar. "On the Economic Theory of Socialism." In Benjamin E. Lippincott, ed., *On the Economic Theory of Socialism*. New York: Augustus M. Kelly, 1970.

Lasswell, Harold and Kaplan, Abraham. *Power and Society*. New Haven: Yale University Press, 1950.

Leoni, Bruno. *Freedom and the Law*. Princeton: D. Van Nostrand, 1961.

Lippincott, Benjamin E., ed. *On the Economic Theory of Socialism*. New York: Augustus M. Kelly, 1970.

"Living Conveniently on the Left." *Time*, June 23, 1980.

Lowi, Theodore J. *The End of Liberalism*. New York: W. W. Norton and Company, 1969.

Lucas, J. R. "Liberty, Morality, and Justice." In Robert L. Cunningham, ed., *Liberty and the Rule of Law*. College Station: Texas A & M University Press, 1979.

Machlup, Fritz, ed., *Essays on Hayek*. New York: New York University Press, 1976a.

Machlup, Fritz. "Hayek's Contribution to Economics." In Fritz Machlup, ed., *Essays on Hayek*. New York: New York University Press, 1976b.

McIlwain, Charles Howard. *Constitutionalism and the Changing World*. New York: The Macmillan Company, 1939.

———. *Constitutionalism: Ancient and Modern*. Ithaca, New York: Cornell University Press, 1947.

Mill, John Stuart. *On Liberty*. Introduction by Currin V. Shields. New York: The Library of Liberal Arts, 1956.

———. *Considerations on Representative Government*. Introduction by Currin V. Shields. New York: The Library of Liberal Arts, 1958.

Miller, Eugene F. "The Cognitive Basis of Hayek's Political Thought." In Robert L. Cunningham, ed., *Liberty and the Rule of Law*. College Station: Texas A & M University Press, 1979.

Minard, Lawrence. "Wave of the Past? Or Wave of the Future?" *Forbes*, October 1, 1979.

Neustadt, Richard. *Presidential Power*. New York: John Wiley and Sons, 1960.

Nozick, Robert. *Anarchy, State, and Utopia*. New York: Basic Books, 1974.

O'Driscoll, Gerald P. *Economics as a Coordination Problem, the Contributions of Friedrich A. Hayek*. Kansas City: Andrews and McMeel, Sheed, 1977.

Olson, Mancur. *The Logic of Collective Action*. Cambridge, Massachusetts: Harvard University Press, 1971.

Plato. *The Republic*. Translated by Francis MacDonald Cornford. New York: Oxford University Press, 1945.

———. *Gorgias*. Translated by Walter Hamilton. Baltimore: Penguin Books, 1960.

Popper, Karl. *The Open Society and Its Enemies*, vol. 1. New York: Harper and Row, 1962.

Price, H. Douglas. "The Electoral Arena." In David Truman, ed. *The Congress and America's Future*. Englewood Cliffs, N.J.: Prentice-Hall, 1965.

Raz, Joseph. "The Rule of Law and Its Virtue." In Robert L. Cunningham, ed., *Liberty and the Rule of Law*, College Station: Texas A & M University Press, 1979.

Rousseau, Jean Jacques. *The Social Contract and Discourses*. Translated by G. D. H. Cole. New York: Dutton and Co., 1950.

Russell, Bertrand. *Power*. New York: W. W. Norton, 1938.

Schlesinger, Jr., Arthur M. *The Imperial Presidency*. New York: Popular Library, 1974.

Schumpeter, Joseph A. *Capitalism, Socialism and Democracy*. New York: Harper and Row, 1950.

Selden, Arthur, ed., *Agenda for a Free Society*. London: The Institute of Economic Affairs, 1961.

Seligman, B. *Main Currents in Modern Economics*. New York: The Free Press of Glencoe, 1962.

Shenfield, A. A. "Law." In Arthur Selden, ed., *Agenda for a Free Society*. London: The Institute of Economic Affairs, 1961.

Tawney, R. H. *The Attack and Other Papers*. London: George Allen and Unwin, 1953.

Taylor, Fred M. "The Guidance of Production in a Socialist State." In Benjamin E. Lippincott, ed., *On the Economic Theory of Socialism*. New York: Augustus M. Kelly, 1970.

Truman, David B. *The Governmental Process*. New York: Alfred A. Knopf, 1971.

Vile, M. J. C. *Constitutionalism and the Separation of Powers*. Oxford: Clarendon Press, 1967.

von Mises, Ludwig. "Economic Calculation in the Socialist Commonwealth." In F. A. Hayek, ed., *Collectivist Economic Planning*. London: George Routledge and Sons, 1935.

———. *Human Action*. New Haven: Yale University Press, 1949.

———. *Socialism*. New Haven: Yale University Press, 1951.

Wallich, Henry C. *The Cost of Freedom*. New York: Collier Books, 1960.

Watkins, J. W. N. "Philosophy." In Arthur Selden, ed., *Agenda for a Free Society*. London: The Institute of Economic Affairs, 1961.

Wilhelm, Morris M. "The Political Philosophy of Friedrich A. Hayek." Ph.D. dissertation, Columbia University, 1969.

———. "The Political Thought of Friedrich A. Hayek. " *Political Studies*, 20, no. 2, 1972.

Wooton, Barbara. *Freedom under Planning*. London: George Allen and Unwin, 1945.

Index

About the Author

CALVIN M. HOY received his Ph.D. from Columbia University. He has taught in the Department of Economics, History, and Government at Union College, Cranford, New Jersey.